ISBN 1-58030-017-0

# If Not Now, When?

Addressing Gender-based Violence in Refugee, Internally Displaced, and Post-conflict Settings

## A Global Overview

*Jeanne Ward*

April, 2002

The Reproductive Health for Refugees Consortium
c/o The Women's Commission for Refugee Women and Children
and the International Rescue Committee
122 East 42nd Street
New York, NY 10168-1289
212.551.3000
www.rhrc.org

# Table of Contents

# List of Frequently Used Acronyms

CEDAW     United Nations Convention on the Elimination of All Forms of Discrimination Against Women

GBV       gender-based violence

IDP       internally displaced person

IOM       International Organization for Migration

IRC       International Rescue Committee

IFRC      International Federation of the Red Cross

MSF       Médecins Sans Frontières

NGO       non-governmental organization

PHR       Physicians for Human Rights

RHRC      Reproductive Health for Refugees Consortium

UNDP      United Nations Development Program

UNFPA     United Nations Population Fund

UNICEF    United Nations Children's Fund

UNIFEM    United Nations Development Fund for Women

UNHCR     United Nations High Commissioner for Refugees

WHO       World Health Organization

# Foreword

This report is one of several outcomes of a two-year global Gender-based Violence Initiative spearheaded by the Reproductive Health for Refugees Consortium (RHRC) and aimed at improving international and local capacity to address gender-based violence (GBV) in refugee, internally displaced, and post-conflict settings. The Initiative was made possible with generous funding by the U.S. Department of State's Bureau of Population, Refugees, and Migration (PRM). The Women's Commission for Refugee Women and Children (Women's Commission) and the International Rescue Committee (IRC) have jointly supervised all aspects of implementing the Initiative.

The overall objective of this report is to provide a baseline narrative account of some of the major issues, programming efforts, and gaps in programming related to the prevention of and response to GBV among conflict-affected populations worldwide. Other outcomes of the Initiative, including an extensive web-based bibliography of GBV resources (accessible at www.rhrc.org/resources/gbv/bib) and an RHRC field manual for GBV assessment, program design, and evaluation, are meant to supplement the findings of this report with practical and field-friendly tools, as well as educational and training materials.

The report is composed of twelve country profiles: three each for Africa, Asia, Europe, and Latin America. Selection of the countries was based on global representation as well as the extent to which they variously represent stages of conflict and types of GBV. Efforts were made not to investigate settings where reviews of GBV-related programming had already been widely published. For practical purposes, countries in Africa, Asia, and Europe with RHRC member field offices available to facilitate site visits were given priority.

Nine profiles—the Republic of Congo, Rwanda, Sierra Leone, Afghanistan/Pakistan, Burma/Thailand, East Timor, Azerbaijan, Bosnia and Herzegovina, and Kosovo—are the outcome of one- to two-week field investigations that included interviews with survivors, local GBV-related organizations, international humanitarian aid and human rights organizations, local and national government representatives, and United Nations personnel. Given the logistical challenges imposed by the brevity of the visits, the findings within each profile are not meant to be exhaustive but, rather, to provide an impression upon which to base further research and programming activities. Moreover, the profiles represent circumstances only as they existed during the period of the site visits, the dates of which are identified at the beginning of each profile and in the annex that follows this report. The one exception to this rule is the profile of Afghanistan/Pakistan, in which consideration was given in the recommendations to the exceptional events that have recently altered the landscape of possibility for instituting GBV-related programming.

The profiles are broadly divided into sections, including background information, GBV issues, GBV-related programming, and recommendations. The background sections exist to provide a general context in which GBV incidents and programming occur, and subsequent sections attempt to be as specific as possible in illustrating the nature and prevalence of GBV, the activities underway, and the gaps in those activities that contribute to the perpetuation of GBV. The recommendations section is without exception based on commentary provided during site visit interviews. However, information in the profiles that originated from personal interviews is generally not cited in order to preserve the confidentiality of those offering their experiences and insights. Information taken from secondary reports is cited in the notes, and these reports have become a part of the RHRC library of GBV information.

The profiles for Colombia, Guatemala, and Nicaragua are the result of New York-based desk studies undertaken during the fall of 2001 by Melinda Leonard, graduate student of the Columbia University School for International and Public Affairs. Resources for the desk studies were primarily published reports and telephone interviews with international and local experts. Since the profiles of Latin America were not informed by site visits (because of changes in project funding), their findings focus on descriptive accounts of available information about GBV issues and programming. While organizations and initiatives have undoubtedly been overlooked in the Latin America profiles given the general difficulty in gaining access to program materials, the profiles nevertheless provide useful overviews for considering GBV prevention and response in the countries under review. They follow the general format of the Africa, Asia, and Europe profiles, with the exception that the specific recommendations generated during site visits are absent from the Latin America profiles.

Although GBV encompasses violence against boys and girls and men and women, the findings of this report focus almost exclusively on violence experienced by women and girls. The reasons for this orientation are two-fold: first, GBV programming targeting men and boy survivors is virtually non-existent among conflict-affected populations; and second, women and girls are the primary targets of GBV worldwide. This report has been produced with the sincere hope that its information will not only stimulate GBV-related programming addressing the particular vulnerabilities of women and girls but also motivate further examination of methods for prevention of and response to GBV that engages boys, girls, men, and women.

## About the Reproductive Health for Refugees Consortium

The Reproductive Health for Refugees Consortium was established in 1995 to promote the institutionalization of reproductive health services in refugee settings worldwide. Consortium members represent a unique mix of advocacy, development, humanitarian relief, research, and training organizations. Four members—the American Refugee Committee, CARE, the International Rescue Committee, and Marie Stopes International—focus on working with international and local NGOs, U.N. agencies, refugees, and host country governments to provide direct reproductive health services to refugees. JSI Research and Training Institute and Columbia University Mailman School of Public Health at the Heilbrunn Department of Population and Family Health are primarily involved in project research, staff training, and technical assistance. The Women's Commission for Refugee Women and Children, as an expert resource and advocacy organization, serves as coordinator of the Consortium. Each member of the Consortium has capacity and experience in gender-based violence research, training, and programming.

# Acknowledgements

The first order of thanks for the information contained in this report goes to all the survivors of GBV around the world who have provided, through their courageous testimony and advocacy, a glimpse of the atrocities that women and girls face not only in periods of conflict but also in flight from conflict, while living in refugee and internally displaced camps, and during post-conflict reconstruction. Their experiences illustrate all too clearly that the perpetration of sexual violence in war—as well as the lack of protective and other services to survivors—is inextricably bound to long-standing gender inequities that contribute to women's and girls' vulnerability to abuse, exploitation, and violence throughout their lives.

Tremendous debt for this report is also owed to all the field-based organizations and individuals who so enthusiastically shared their GBV-related expertise, and who were forthcoming with frustrations about addressing GBV in political and socio-cultural climates that more often marginalize the issue. Though the list of contributors is too exhaustive to enumerate here, many of their activities are mentioned within the narrative of each country profile, and their perspectives underpin all the recommendations set forth in this report.

Thanks are similarly due to the local government, United Nations, and international human rights and aid organization representatives who tirelessly extended themselves during my site visits in Africa, Asia, and Europe. Their generous assistance and referrals added immeasurably to my understanding of each of the countries under investigation. I was a privileged recipient of their expert knowledge and, in many cases, their considerable hospitality.

Suzanne Petroni, formerly of PRM, participated in the trip to Azerbaijan and not only offered her wisdom—the result of her long-standing commitment to confronting and reducing violence against women—but also provided helpful feedback on the Azerbaijan profile. Cari Clark, a doctoral student at the Harvard School of Public Health, joined the trip to Azerbaijan, as well as to Kosovo and Bosnia and Herzegovina. Her special knowledge of and interest in GBV research methodologies were an important contribution to the site visits, as were her patience and flexibility. Her ongoing efforts to improve GBV-related research will undoubtedly serve those who are engaged in addressing GBV among conflict-affected populations. Betsy Kovacs, a board member of the Women's Commission, was an enthusiastic participant in the trip to Bosnia and Herzegovina. Her dedication and intelligence were great assets during the site visit, and her subsequent friendship and insights have assisted me not only in writing the Bosnia and Herzegovina country profile, but also in conceptualizing some of the larger issues that inform this entire report.

Members of RHRC assisted in numerous ways—facilitating site visits, providing expert background information, and reviewing individual country profiles. Sandra Krause of the Women's Commission and Mary Otieno of the IRC are in large part responsible for this report—through the ongoing provision of guidance and recommendations, as well as through a revolving door of support. Beth Vann, the Gender-based Violence Technical Advisor to the RHRC, has been a comrade and collaborator, sharing a level of expertise essential to my understanding of GBV in conflict-affected settings.

A number of individuals read the country profiles on Asia, Africa, and Europe, and many provided critical feedback on content and organization. Sandra Krause deserves special credit for commenting on all the profiles. Mary Otieno provided important insights about the overall structure of the report. Paul Ward, Sr. lent his editorial expertise to several of the profiles. The Republic of Congo profile was reviewed by Mary Otieno and Les Roberts of IRC Headquarters. Lizanne McBride of IRC Rwanda, Huy Pham of the American Refugee Committee (ARC) Headquarters, and Mary Balikingeri of the Rwanda Women's Network offered feedback for the Rwanda profile. Sierra Leone was enhanced by comments from Martha Saldinger of ARC Sierra Leone, Marnie Glaeberman, formerly with IRC's GBV program in Sierra Leone, Samantha Guy of Marie Stopes International, and the Women's Commission's Sierra Leone-based field officer Binta Mansaray. Afghanistan/Pakistan was supplemented by recommendations from Ramina Johal of the Women's Commission, as well as from Colleen McGinn, former GBV research consultant for IRC Pakistan. Burma/Thailand was thoughtfully edited by Gary Dahl of ARC Thailand, and recommendations were offered as well by Lori Bell of IRC Thailand and Huy Pham. Richard Brennan of IRC Headquarters made contributions to the East Timor profile, as did Carmen Lowry, former program manager for IRC's East Timor GBV program. Azerbaijan benefited from the critical commentary of Mominat Omarova, Vice Chairperson of the State Committee on Women's Issues, Suzanne Petroni and Cari Clark. Zeljka Mudrovcic of the United Nations Population Fund in Bosnia and Herzegovina, and Betsy Kovacs, Samantha Guy and Cari Clark provided important recommendations for Bosnia and Herzegovina.

The desk study overviews representing countries in Latin America are the result of Melinda Leonard's undaunted commitment to the challenging task of writing profiles without having conducted site visits. She was assisted in identifying GBV projects and programs by international and field-based experts, including Deborah Billings of IPAS in Mexico City, Alessandra Guedes of the International Planned Parenthood Federation in New York, Oswaldo Montoya and Patrick Welsh of the Association of Men Against Violence in Nicaragua, and Sandra Krause. Claire Morris of Marie Stopes International and Patricia Ospina Mayorga and Ana Vega of Profamilia Colombia offered helpful feedback on the Colombia profile.

Mary Murrell has extended her expertise to the review of this entire report. Her generous friendship has been as important to the editorial process as her considerable professional skill.

Bruce Ward, for reasons too innumerable to mention, is fundamental to the existence of this report.

Finally, this report would not have been possible without the generous financial assistance of PRM. Their commitment to addressing GBV issues among conflict-affected populations has significantly advanced GBV prevention and response activities in refugee and internally displaced settings. PRM's support of this global overview further illustrates their dedication to expanding the knowledge base upon which effective programming can be designed.

# Executive Summary

## Introduction

Throughout history, gender-based violence has been an integral component of armed conflict. In the last century, to cite a few examples, Jewish women were raped by Cossacks during the 1919 pogroms in Russia; the Japanese army sexually enslaved and raped thousands of Korean, Indonesian, Chinese, and Filipino "comfort women" during World War II; and hundreds of thousands of Bengali women were raped by Pakistani soldiers during the 1971 Bangladeshi wars of secession. This report attests to GBV against women and girls (and to a lesser extent men and boys) that has been and continues to be a feature of virtually all recently concluded and current armed conflicts.

Until the last ten years, most GBV committed during periods of armed conflict has been either condoned or ignored. This silence is in significant measure a function of deeply embedded cultural assumptions that acquiesce to the "inevitability" of violence and exploitation of women and girls. Nevertheless, recent interrelated events on the international stage have brought GBV in armed conflict, as well as in refugee, internally displaced, and post-conflict settings, into starker relief. In the broadest terms, these events include: 1) the rise of women's and human rights movements across the world, which have not only identified violence against women as a global phenomenon but have also characterized that violence as an affront to basic human rights; 2) the shift in the nature and scope of humanitarian aid afforded conflict-affected populations, including attention to

the distinct protection needs of women and children and the ascendancy of reproductive health programming; 3) the increased dominance of international legal instruments and institutions in promoting and reinforcing international standards of human rights as they apply both to women and to conflict; 4) the advances in global technology as well as changes in attitudes toward war that have altered the nature of war propaganda and reporting, leading to significant international press coverage of sexual violence during the Bosnia, Rwanda, and Kosovo conflicts; and 5) a basic change in the character of war during the latter half of the past century from military engagements primarily between fighting forces to violence that targets, dislocates, or otherwise victimizes civilian populations.

The stimulus for GBV, particularly sexual crimes, committed in periods of armed conflict varies. Sexual violence can be capricious or random—the "spoils of war"—resulting from the breakdown in social and moral systems. Indeed, it is likely that this kind of "collateral" GBV is an element of all wars. In addition, sexual violence may be systematic, for the purposes of destabilizing populations and destroying bonds within communities and families; advancing ethnic cleansing; expressing hatred for the enemy; or supplying combatants with sexual services. In Bosnia, for example, public rapes of women and girls preceded the flight or expulsion of entire Muslim populations from their towns or villages, and strategies of ethnic cleansing included forced impregnation. East Timorese men were forced to rape women in the presence of the Indonesian military, and East

Timorese women were raped in the presence of family members. Some were raped because of their assumed link to the East Timorese resistance; others were forced into prostitution servicing Indonesian troops. In Rwanda, Hutu extremists encouraged mass rape and sexual mutilation of Tutsi women as an expression of contempt that sometimes included intentional HIV transmission. Under the volatile and disorganized rule of the Mujahideen, rape and sexual harassment of women in Afghanistan's capital city of Kabul were reportedly commonplace, and in the years following the Taliban takeover, ethnic minority women in the frontlines of combat were at risk of rape and abduction by all parties to the conflict. In Sierra Leone and Burma, rebel, paramilitary, and military contingents force women and girls into sexual slavery and, in some cases, marriage. Sexual crimes also occur in flight from conflict and during civilian displacement, committed by bandits, insurgency groups, military, border guards, host communities, humanitarian aid workers, security or peacekeeping forces, and fellow refugees.

Whether indiscriminate or methodical, sexual violence is only one variation of GBV that periods of armed conflict and consequent social disruption exacerbate. Other forms of violence that may increase during war and its aftermath include: early or forced marriage, especially in cultures with traditions of early marriage and dowry; female infanticide; enforced sterilization; domestic violence, which in virtually all post-conflict settings is acknowledged as a component of the "culture of violence" that ensues from war; forced or coerced prostitution or other forms of sexual exploitation, often an outcome of the disproportionate impact of war-related poverty on women and girls; and trafficking in women and girls, to which the black markets that invariably attend conflict appear to give rise. Forced conscription of boys—based on assumptions of males' responsibility to take up arms—is also a common and immeasurably devastating component of many current conflicts. All these manifestations of GBV, as well as others that may not significantly increase during conflict but are nevertheless the outcome of harmful traditional practices, such as female genital cutting and honor killing, are based on customary attitudes and behaviors that sustain and reinforce gender-based abuse and exploitation, not only in times of war but also in periods of so-called peace.

# Gender-based Violence Programming

## Definition of Terms

Women's rights research, advocacy, and practice have produced a dynamic and evolving discourse that frames how international humanitarian institutions and organizations have conceptualized violence against women and girls in conflict-affected settings. These conceptualizations have contributed to changes in the GBV-related idiom of the humanitarian community. One of the earliest GBV-specific projects of the United Nations High Commissioner for Refugees (UNHCR), instituted in 1993 in refugee camps in northern Kenya, was entitled the "Women Victims of Violence Project." In 1995 UNHCR published *Sexual Violence Against Refugees: Guidelines on Prevention and Response.* As with the Kenya program, its focus was primarily on sexual violence, primarily as perpetrated against women. The International Rescue Committee's (IRC) first GBV initiative, launched in refugee camps in Tanzania in 1996, was entitled the "Sexual and Gender-based Violence Program." Gender was overtly recognized as elemental to violence, even if sexual violence remained a separate manifestation that, implicit in the phraseology, was not necessarily gendered. Beginning in 2001, the Reproductive Health for Refugees Consortium (RHRC) has advocated for the inclusion of sexual violence under the umbrella term "gender-based violence" so to recognize that issues of gender underlie virtually all forms violence against women and girls that humanitarian programming seeks to address. As such, newer initiatives are more succinctly referred to as "gender-based violence programs." The centrality of gender has important theoretical and practical implications for anti-violence activities: the language itself speaks to the necessity of examining the societal and relational contexts in which violence against women and girls occurs, and therefore begs the inclusion of men, women, boys, and girls.

*Gender* refers to the attributes and roles differentially ascribed to males and females. These attributes and roles are socially constructed, context based, and learned through socialization. Although mutable, they are rooted in long-standing assumptions societies hold about women, men, boys, and girls. They inform relationships between males and females as well as among females and among males.

*Gender-based violence* is an umbrella term for any harm

that is perpetrated against a person's will; that has a negative impact on the physical or psychological health, development, and identity of the person; and that is the result of gendered power inequities that exploit distinctions between males and females, among males, and among females. Although not exclusive to women and girls, GBV principally affects them across all cultures. Violence may be physical, sexual, psychological, economic, or sociocultural. Categories of perpetrators may include family members, community members, and those acting on behalf of or in proportion to the disregard of cultural, religious, state, or intrastate institutions.

Any analysis of or attempt to reduce GBV must necessarily examine and confront the gendered foundations upon which violence occurs. It should be noted, however, that even though gender is one of the most significant factors *around the world* in the perpetuation of violence against women and girls, other essential criteria for evaluating and addressing the nature and prevalence of violence include class, race, poverty level, ethnicity, and age.

## GBV and Human Rights

Focusing on the contexts in which violence occurs is crucial to reducing violence, but there remains in the international humanitarian aid community a fear of imposing "western" standards of social organization and behavior on disparate refugee, internally displaced, and post-conflict populations across the world. During research for this report, for example, many international representatives of the humanitarian aid community expressed the opinion that acts of GBV were the preserve of culture and therefore outside the scope of humanitarian intervention. This perspective may itself be paternalistic in its failure to acknowledge local communities' desire to improve the rights of its own members, but at the same time its concerns are rooted in a respect for difference that should be a feature of all humanitarian work. Nonetheless, when applied to GBV, this reluctance to intervene may reinforce behaviors that hurt and kill women and girls and, by extension, destroy families and societies.

The efforts of human rights activists (including women's rights activists) have informed deeply the work of humanitarian aid in conflict-affected populations. The premise of equal access to human rights is basic to the humanitarian agenda. Furthermore,

when extended to humanitarian interventions, the human rights perspective demands that those interventions are by nature participatory—that is, they engage at every level of program assessment, design, implementation, and evaluation with the communities the programming is intended to assist. In terms of GBV programming, a human rights approach both insists that GBV is addressed within the context of humanitarian assistance and that any efforts to confront GBV are inclusive of the population served and squarely rooted in the needs identified by those most vulnerable.

Even so, there are settings around the world—by no means exclusive to conflict-affected populations—where complacency regarding certain types of GBV is the norm, both for perpetrators and victims. Men and women alike, for example, may agree that husbands are entitled to beat their wives. Perhaps even more common to conflict-affected populations, human rights are often viewed as non-essential luxuries when there is little or no access to water, food, or shelter. However, as the findings of this and other reports illustrate, those most at risk on *all counts* in refugee, internally displaced, and post-conflict settings are women and children. Their disproportionate vulnerability is informed by their subordinate status. Thus, any framework for humanitarian action must use the language and the perspective of human rights *and* gender equality if the most vulnerable are to be assisted.

Acts of GBV violate a number of principles enshrined in international and regional human rights instruments. A partial list of those principles includes the right to life, equality, security of the person, equal protection under the law, and freedom from torture and other cruel, inhumane, or degrading treatment. The Convention on the Elimination of All Forms of Discrimination Against Women (ratified by the United Nations in 1979), to which *all countries represented in this report* have acceded, commits its signatories to condemn violence against women, to create legal and social protections against violence, and not to invoke custom, tradition, or religion to avoid the obligations it outlines. The Declaration on the Elimination of Violence Against Women, adopted by the U.N. General Assembly in 1993, and the subsequent Global Platform for Action, adopted at the Beijing Fourth World Conference on Women in 1995, further elaborate the nature of GBV and reiterate state responsibility to protect women and girls.

In 1998 the International Criminal Court adopted the Rome Statute, which defines crimes against humanity to include torture, rape, sexual slavery, enforced prostitution, forced pregnancy, enforced sterilization, or any other comparably grave acts of sexual violence that are committed as part of a systematic attack on civilian populations. The International Criminal Tribunals for Rwanda and the former Yugoslavia have each handed down sentences that characterize sexual violence committed against women during conflict, respectively, as crimes of genocide (1998) and as crimes against humanity (2001). In 2000, the U.N. Security Council adopted Resolution 1325, which specifically "calls upon all parties to armed conflict to take special measures to protect women and girls from gender-based violence, particularly rape and other forms of sexual abuse, and all other forms of violence in situations of armed conflict."

Protecting the rights of conflict-affected populations is at the heart of the responsibilities of international humanitarian response. UNHCR's *Guidelines on the Protection of Refugee Women* (1991) recognized exposure to sexual violence as a particular vulnerability of refugee women and called upon the humanitarian community to address it within its protection mandate, and in 1995 UNHCR released its *Sexual Violence Against Refugees: Guidelines on Prevention and Response*, which more explicitly highlighted some of the major legal, medical, and psychosocial components of GBV prevention and response.

## GBV and Reproductive Health

Although the *Guidelines on the Protection of Refugee Women* and the subsequent *Sexual Violence Against Refugees: Guidelines on Prevention and Response* were each important in identifying violence against women as components of conflict and displacement, these guidelines did not promote methodologies for developing specific field-based programs or protocols to tackle GBV. And although there were several model GBV programs instituted for conflict-affected populations before the mid-1990s—which addressed, for example, domestic violence among Cambodian refugees and sexual violence in Liberia and among refugees in northern Kenya—there was no attempt to standardize GBV activities until international reproductive health advocates incorporated GBV within their mandate. In 1994, the Women's Commission for Refugee Women and Children released a groundbreaking study, *Refugee Women and Reproductive Health:*

*Reassessing Priorities*, that revealed even the most basic reproductive health services—including those to address GBV—were not available to refugee and displaced women. Following the precedent-setting 1994 International Conference on Population and Development in Cairo, and with strong support from an influential donor base, reproductive health was introduced in humanitarian settings. In expanding minimum health standards for refugees and IDPs, GBV was recognized as a major factor in women's morbidity and mortality. The significance of this change in health programming cannot be underestimated: it was through the portal of reproductive health that GBV programming was widely introduced into conflict-affected populations.

In 1995 UNHCR and the United Nations Population Fund (UNFPA) collaborated to form an Inter-Agency Working Group (IAWG) of expert international reproductive health organizations. A year later IAWG produced an inter-agency field manual, *Reproductive Health in Refugee Situations*, that includes information about the prevention and management of GBV from the emergency to stable phase of displacement. The manual was field-tested and reproduced in 1999.

RHRC has integrated GBV as a technical area within reproductive health training and services; as such, all the services advocated for and (at least theoretically) provided by the RHRC have a GBV component. In 1995, CARE took over from UNHCR its "Women Victims of Violence Project" in refugee camps in Kenya. Since then, the lead RHRC agency in addressing GBV has been IRC, which in 1996 initiated its Tanzania program and from there has established at least twelve GBV programs worldwide. RHRC's other direct service members, ARC and Marie Stopes International, have also targeted GBV in their programming. Other international organizations working in humanitarian contexts that have incorporated GBV within their programming include the International Medical Corps, OXFAM, Save the Children, Médecins Sans Frontières, and the Christian Children's Fund.

## Current Standards for GBV Prevention and Response

The intersection of reproductive health and GBV allowed for a greater understanding of and greater attention to the physical and mental health impacts of GBV, including sexually transmitted infections, reproductive tract trauma, unwanted pregnancy and complications associated with unsafe abortions, somatic complaints, depression, and suicide. However, the focal point of reproductive health resulted in GBV programming that was often based on the provision of curative services, such that other aspects of GBV programming were given short shrift in humanitarian settings. Furthermore, sexual violence was the primary element of early programming, even as other forms of GBV were being identified by service providers. In 1998, UNHCR received $1.65 million from the U.N. Foundation to strengthen its ability to address GBV in Africa. As programs multiplied and reports were published and disseminated, UNHCR and its implementing international and local NGO partners recognized that any attempts to address GBV—both in terms of prevention and response—must be the outcome of coordinated activities between the constituent community, health and social services, and the legal and security sectors. In 2001, UNHCR hosted an international conference on GBV, in which the concept of multisectoral programming was further clarified as fundamental to combating GBV. To date, this multisectoral model forms the "best practice" for prevention of and response to GBV in refugee, IDP, and post-conflict settings.

The underlying principle of the multisectoral model recognizes the rights and needs of survivors as preeminent, in terms of access to respectful and supportive services, guarantees of confidentiality and safety, and the ability to determine a course of action for addressing the GBV incident. Key characteristics of the multisectoral model include the full engagement of the refugee community, interdisciplinary and interorganizational cooperation, and collaboration and coordination among sectors. Within the heath sector, participating actors might include health facility staff, doctors, nurses, midwives, traditional birth attendants, community health workers, traditional health practitioners, health managers, administrators, and health ministry officials and staff. In the social services sector, actors might include UNHCR community services officers, community volunteers, social workers, teachers and school administrators, skills training program managers and staff, income generation and micro-credit program managers and staff, and representatives of the ministry attending to social welfare. Within the legal sector, actors might be UNHCR protection officers/assistants, judges and other officers of the court, legislators, lawyers, NGOs and legal advocacy groups, and representatives of the country's equivalent of a Ministry of Justice. The security sector might include police, peacekeeping forces, international and national military, security and field officers in UNHCR and NGOs, and representatives of the Ministry of the Interior. And of course, if existent, any multisectoral collaboration would involve close cooperation with local women's groups and representatives from the ministry responsible for addressing the needs of women and girls.

Each of these sectors is charged under the multisectoral model with basic responsibilities related to the prevention of and response to GBV. The health sector, for example, should be able to: actively screen clients for GBV in a way that is respectful and supportive; ensure same sex interviewers for survivors; respond to the immediate health and psychological needs of the survivor, and, wherever possible, provide those services free of cost. Health care providers should also be prepared to collect forensic evidence when authorized by the survivor and provide testimony in cases where a survivor chooses to pursue legal action; be aware of and refer survivors to other support services; confidentially collect, document, and analyze health data and data on the quality of services, so as to adjust services accordingly; and provide broad-based community education on the health impacts of GBV and the availability of services.

The social services sector should be able to: provide supportive and ongoing psychological assistance, in which social workers and community services workers have access to professional supervision and support; confidentially collect, document, and analyze client care data, and adjust programming accordingly; offer safe haven for victims who choose to leave an unsafe environment; provide hotlines—in settings where phones exist—to facilitate support and referral; offer income generation and training programs that allow women and girls sustained economic viability; conduct broad-based community education on the prevention of GBV and on the availability of services; and provide early childhood and adolescent education about safe touch, gender, and healthy relationships.

Members of the legal sector should work to: review and revise laws that reinforce GBV and gender discrimination; provide free or low-cost legal counseling and representation to survivors; conduct ongoing training to members of the judiciary to apply GBV laws and carry out judicial proceedings privately, respectfully, and safely; institute provisions for monitoring court processes and collecting and analyzing data on cases; and conduct broad-based community education on the existence and content of anti-GBV laws.

Within the security sector, a zero tolerance policy should exist for all police, military, and peacekeeping staff who contribute to or commit acts of GBV, and that policy should be actively enforced by those in command. The security sector should be trained and prepared to intervene in cases of GBV in a way that acknowledges the severity of GBV and does not further victimize the survivor by: designating private meeting rooms within police stations; providing same sex police officers to work with survivors; creating specialized units to address various manifestations of GBV, such as sexual violence, domestic violence, and trafficking; offering survivors referrals for collateral assistance; conducting community policing and education programs; instituting ongoing training and supervision of police personnel; and standardizing sex-disaggregated data collection and analysis. Other security personnel should similarly be trained and equipped to intervene in cases of GBV respectfully and in such a manner that "does no harm." In demobilization and reintegration programs for former combatants, anti-GBV education should be integral, as should drug and alcohol counseling.

A critical responsibility of all the sectors is coordination, which within the U.N. refers to the systematic use of policy instruments to deliver humanitarian assistance in a cohesive and effective manner. Coordination includes strategic planning, gathering data and managing information, mobilizing resources and ensuring accountability, orchestrating a functional division of labor, negotiating and maintaining a serviceable framework of action, and providing leadership. At the more prosaic level of institutionalizing programming for GBV prevention and response, coordination includes: sharing information about GBV incident data; discussion and problem-solving among actors about prevention and response activities; and collaborative monitoring, evaluation, and ongoing program planning and development. As part of coordination, methods should exist for reporting and referrals among and between different sectors, and those methods should be continuously monitored

and reviewed. Referral networks should focus on providing prompt, confidential, and appropriate services to survivors. And, perhaps most importantly, regular meetings should be convened involving representatives of the various sectors tasked with GBV responsibilities. A designated "lead agency"—which ideally would be a ministry or other national body but could also be an international institution or organization, or a local NGO or representative body invested with due authority—would be responsible for encouraging participation and facilitating meetings and other methods for coordination and information sharing among sectors.

## An Overview of Findings Contained in This Report

The ideals of multisectoral programming remain just that: ideals. Although GBV prevention and response has been increasingly acclaimed as an important component of humanitarian assistance, that commitment is still not widely realized. In pockets of Bosnia and Herzegovina, such as Zenica and Gorazde, multisectoral coordination initiated by the local GBV programs has engaged the police, health services, and social workers, with apparently good outcomes in facilitating reporting and reducing GBV. More often, programs themselves have adopted an internal multisectoral expertise in order to meet the various needs of survivors, typically providing a mixture of health, psychosocial, and legal support. Most often, though, there are significant gaps in policy, programming, coordination, and protection across all sectors.

Perhaps one of the primary gaps is the lack of data on GBV. In none of the countries represented in this report were service data collected across sectors, either at the local or national level. In many countries, little or no research had been conducted on the prevalence of GBV. In some countries where prevalence research has been conducted, such as Sierra Leone, Azerbaijan, and Kosovo, the findings—though important in their own right as a way to improve awareness of the nature and scope of GBV—were not attached to programming and thus did not directly inform prevention and response activities. In several cases where data were collected by GBV programs, whether through service statistics or prevalence research, the findings resulted in sustained shifts in policy. The Republic of Congo, for example, included sexual violence response as a component of its national health policy following data collection spearheaded by IRC and its partners, and the Ministry of Health now collects sexual violence data from hospitals and clinics where rape-related services have been instituted.

Yet another gap in addressing GBV is the tendency of donors and humanitarian institutions and organizations to focus on sexual crimes committed during conflict. Although establishing services for rape survivors is critical, addressing rape is just one component of GBV programming. In Rwanda, virtually all GBV services focus on the outcomes of genocidal rape—in terms of health provision, psychosocial support, and legal aid—even when prostitution (with related high rates of HIV) and domestic violence are believed to be endemic in the post-genocide society. This is also true of the Republic of Congo, where treating sexual violence has become standardized (at least in Congo's capital city of Brazzaville), but other forms of GBV receive virtually no attention. In few countries has programming reflected the extensive nature of GBV or begun to address its underlying causes.

Protections for survivors of all forms of GBV are weak in every country profiled in this report. This is perhaps most true of unregistered refugees in Thailand and Pakistan, where the lack of host government recognition, the culture of violence against women that supports impunity for GBV-related crimes, and the extreme discrimination against women in general conspire to promote GBV crimes. However, lack of protection is also an element among encamped and post-conflict populations. International security and peacekeeping forces are overwhelmingly male, as are national police and security forces, and very few have had training on preventing GBV or responding to GBV-related reports. UNHCR's ability to provide sustained protection for survivors is all too often only as good as a host country's commitment to addressing the issue, and UNHCR has not widely assumed the important task of advocating to national governments for improved protections in cases of GBV.

One difficulty in ensuring protections is due to variations in GBV-related policy and practice. Although codes of conduct and zero tolerance policies have been instituted for international forces in Bosnia and Herzegovia and Kosovo—particularly with regard to crimes related to prostitution and

trafficking—the will to enforce those codes varies considerably. The commitment to enforcing national laws regarding GBV also varies considerably: while Colombia, for example, has model legislation, GBV is a pervasive and largely ignored problem. Very often, the judiciary is simply left out of the equation when developing training and protocols for improved response to GBV. This omission was apparent in both the Guatemalan Ministry of Public Health's research and a report by the Organization for Security and Cooperation in Europe, which revealed biases within Kosovo's judicial system that severely inhibited fair prosecution of GBV cases.

Even so, successes such as the high percentage of women recruited into the Kosovo Police Services and the trainings conducted by international personnel for East Timor's national police cadets are models for implementing ongoing protection. So are the efforts of a senior Sierra Leone police officer and a Kosovo international police officer, who established domestic violence units in their respective police headquarters; and an international police officer based in East Timor who established systems of disaggregated data collection on reported cases of violence.

Short-term funding and shifting donor priorities have also contributed to the inability of many programs to achieve the degree of expertise and conduct the level of comprehensive activities required to adequately combat GBV. To a remarkable extent in many of the post-conflict settings profiled in this report, local women's organizations have quickly regrouped or newly formed to address issues of GBV. However, because funding for conflict-affected populations is generally limited to emergency response, and because there are gaps between "emergency" relief and "development" programming, many organizations that might build on their preexisting knowledge of and commitment to GBV programming often diversify their activities and mandates to meet changing donor expectations.

Moreover, the notion of self-sustainability, which is a central requirement of many donor initiatives, is generally unrealistic as it applies to GBV programming. In post-conflict settings where national and local economies are more often too weak to support social services (and where GBV issues are marginalized in any case), it is almost a given that GBV programs will not be able to access sufficient ongoing local funding. They should not then also be expected to add income-generation to their tasks. One particularly disturbing case in point was the hotline that was established in Gorazde, Bosnia and Herzegovina. The community considered the existence of the hotline to be an important resource for women and for the local police and social workers with whom the hotline collaborated, but lack of funding caused the hotline to be precipitously shut down. Another example is the well-regarded Women's Wellness Center in Pejë, Kosovo. Even though the center had a six-month transition period from being supported by an international NGO to establishing itself as an independent local NGO, at the end of those six months the center's director had only identified an additional six months of funding, and even that was insufficient to cover staff salaries. Overall multisectoral integration of GBV prevention and response activities should be a goal for any donor or implementing agency; however, integration requires ongoing monitoring and support from institutions and organizations—such as the Women's Wellness Center—that are specifically charged with and expert in addressing GBV. Invariably, the most successful and sustained programs are those that receive long-term technical and financial assistance from international donors committed to issues of women's rights and GBV reduction. A model example is Medica Zenica in Bosnia and Herzegovina, and its primary donor, Medica Mondiale. Kvinna till Kvinna has also been a tremendous source of funding and support to women's organizations throughout the war-affected Balkans. The U.S. Department of State's Bureau of Population, Refugees, and Migration has not only funded this report, but has in the last several years made an exemplary impact on GBV programming by supporting international research, global technical assistance, and field-based programming.

Lack of national-level strategies or policies to address GBV also contributes to the failure of broad-based programming and coordination. In part this lack of national recognition regarding GBV can be attributed to the general lack of representation of women in positions of influence. In post-conflict settings, it also speaks to the failures in international- and national-level planning to anticipate GBV as an important area for attention in any reconstruction efforts. In most of the countries represented in this report, there are no government-supported mechanisms for coordination specific to GBV. As a result, GBV programs have often developed vertically, independent of the cross-cutting sectors that could provide broad support in the prevention of and response to GBV. In many cases, GBV programs have also developed independent of other in-country international and local GBV programs. If coordination does occur, it is often from the efforts of a motivated individual or organization, often working outside a specific mandate, whose reach is limited by lack of resources and institutional support.

Because addressing the gender inequities that contribute to GBV is fundamental to addressing the perpetuation of GBV, any programming that seeks to reduce GBV must also challenge the social, cultural, and political determinants of violence. Such programming requires a long-term commitment to awareness-raising and advocacy, as well as recognition that addressing GBV includes providing women and girls access to power. Inasmuch as GBV programming should be integrated across sectors, so should efforts at gender mainstreaming. However, it is more often the case that international institutions and organizations, even if they theoretically support women's empowerment as a goal of programming, do not challenge the structures that reinforce women's subordination. To a certain extent this is exemplified in the Women's Initiatives in Bosnia, Rwanda, and Kosovo. A laudable goal of each initiative was to support the empowerment of women, but that goal often translated into small-scale income generation projects, which in some cases may have exacerbated, rather than reduced, the feminization of poverty that is often an outcome of conflict. Notably, none of the Initiatives had overt strategies for addressing GBV prevention and response as a component of women's empowerment.

With the exception of the model initiatives in Nicaragua and the White Ribbon Campaigns in the Balkans, men are essentially absent, both as targets for services and as agents for change, from GBV programming represented in this report. Although several GBV programs in Africa and the Balkans are staffed with men, and although community education does not exclude men, most often GBV-related activities focus on women and girls as potential victims and as survivors. This orientation to women and girls as service recipients justly reflects the reality of women and girls as the primary victims of GBV. However, any efforts to reduce GBV will require the significant participation of men and boys and must necessarily include activities and initiatives to examine men's participation in, and perpetuation of, violence.

## Overview of Recommendations Contained in This Report

1. The donor community should examine its commitment to addressing the health and safety needs of refugee, internally displaced, and post-conflict populations; and, acknowledging the human rights violations and major impact of GBV on morbidity and mortality, pledge resources to institutionalize broad-based health and other support services to assist survivors, as well as initiatives to reduce the prevalence of GBV. Short-term self-sustainability should not be a requisite of donor support. Priority funding should be given to expert local NGOs that can assist national and local governments to institutionalize plans and protocols to address GBV.

2. National governments should review their charge of protecting refugees and internally displaced, and ensure that the same degree of protection accorded the general population also applies to refugee and IDP populations. On this basis, improvements in addressing GBV should be relevant to all those under government jurisdiction.

3. Broad-based programs to address GBV in refugee and IDP settings should be designed and implemented proactively. Protocols should exist to anticipate, identify, and prevent GBV. Multisectoral response should be integrated into refugee and IDP communities from the outset of U.N. intervention, with the full participation of refugee communities, especially those most vulnerable. Wherever possible, experts from the host community should be engaged to provide GBV training and service delivery.

4. National and local governments, in collaboration with U.N. institutions and international and local implementing partners and local women's representatives, should institutionalize coordination of multisectoral GBV prevention and response activities. Any coordinating body initially led by the U.N. or its implementing partners should have a long-term plan for transitioning to national government oversight.

5. Confidential data collection should be standardized within sectors, as should methods for data sharing across sectors. Data should be monitored, evaluated and integrated at the local and national level.

6. International peacekeeping and security forces should improve their monitoring of personnel who may directly or inadvertently contribute to coerced or forced prostitution, sexual exploitation, trafficking, and other forms of GBV, holding them to international codes of conduct and the responsibilities outlined in U.N. Security Council Resolution 1325. Females should be actively recruited to international security and peacekeeping forces.

7. Ministries responsible for internal affairs and the judiciary should require training within their respective sectors on the existence of protective laws related to GBV. Where laws offer inadequate protection, they should be revised. All actors should be held responsible for the application of those laws. Females should be actively recruited to police, military, and the judiciary. Demobilization and reintegration activities should include GBV prevention and response in their education and direct services, as well as psychological and drug abuse counseling.

8. Ministries for social welfare should ensure that GBV prevention and response is an integrated component of social welfare, including education, skills-building, and psychosocial care. Those who provide counseling to survivors should have access to ongoing supervision and support. Wherever possible, shelters and hot-lines should be available. Education and social service programs should reach children and adolescents on issues of safe touch, gender, and healthy relationships.

9. Ministries of health should require that health services include protocols for addressing GBV. Standard training on all aspects of GBV treatment and response should be required for health workers, and the rights of the survivor to safety, confidentiality, and choice should be paramount in any service provision. Services for sexual assault survivors should be free of charge. Confidential data should be collected by clinics and hospitals and monitored, evaluated, and utilized at the institutional, local, and government level.

10. Widespread multi-media campaigns that utilize television, radio, and print should be used to conduct prevention campaigns and to inform survivors about the availability of health, social services, and legal aid in all refugee, IDP, and post-conflict communities.

11. Men's organizations, churches, and governments should be used to involve men and male community representatives in GBV prevention efforts. Models from Latin America, particularly the men's associations in Nicaragua that work to reduce violence against women by confronting issues of masculinity and aggression, should inform efforts to engage men in GBV prevention in other parts of the world.

## Looking to the Future

UNHCR first formally introduced GBV programming into a refugee setting in 1993, and from there prevention and response activities have grown significantly. This growth is a testament to the possibility of confronting GBV. There are important newer initiatives underway that have great promise in advancing global efforts to address GBV in conflict-affected settings. Among those initiatives is a GBV assessment, design, and evaluation manual currently being developed by the RHRC according to the work of RHRC member agencies, especially RHRC's GBV Technical Advisor and its Research Officer. Another important initiative is that of the World Health Organization to standardize medical management guidelines for responding to rape, for which they have designed and are currently field testing a manual. UNHCR is also currently revising its 1995 *Sexual Violence Against Refugees: Guidelines on Prevention and Response* to reflect lessons learned about the importance of multisectoral programming. A GBV-related step-by-step guide for UNHCR protection officers is currently in draft form. The Women's Commission for Refugee Women and Children has undertaken an assessment of the implementation of UNHCR's *Guidelines on the Protection of Refugee Women* and its policy on refugee women; the assessment, to be released in 2002, makes recommendations for improving strategies to address GBV. The Center for Health and Gender Equity, a reproductive health and rights advocacy organization, has created a directory of more than 250 organizations around the world working to integrate GBV and reproductive health, and is developing a

health- and rights-based framework to identify critical elements related to the design, implementation and evaluation of integrated GBV and reproductive health programs in a myriad of contexts. International Medical Corps has retained a technical advisor to assist its health programs in the integration of GBV. Save the Children is currently working on a GBV education manual for its staff. UNFPA has produced a manual for integrating GBV into reproductive health services in development contexts, of which an adaptation for refugee settings is planned. The International Planned Parenthood Federation is supporting several projects in Latin America also aimed at GBV integration and produces *Basta!*, a resource periodical based on its work.

As impressive as these initiatives are, it is the effort of the local communities represented in this report that illustrate the greatest potential for combating GBV in refugee, IDP, and post-conflict settings. As this report illustrates, repeatedly and across cultures inspiration for change is based in local women's unrelenting commitment to reducing the violence that has overwhelmed their communities and their lives.

Country Profiles from Africa

*Republic of Congo*
*Rwanda*
*Sierra Leone*

# Post-Conflict Situation in the *Republic of Congo*

January 22-31, 2001

## Background

### Historical Context

The Republic of Congo (hereafter referred to as Congo) lies in the western shadow of its imposing and fractious neighbor, the Democratic Republic of Congo (formerly Zaire, hereafter DRC). To the south, where the Congo meets the Atlantic Ocean, it shares a small portion of its border with Angola. Both neighbors are engaged in seemingly intractable conflicts, DRC as the central African repository for regional conflict, and Angola as the site of a civil war notable for its human rights violations. Against this backdrop, and following a decade in which widespread killing, torture, rape, and detention of Congolese civilians were the norm, the Congo entered the new millennium in a state of relative peace and stability.

In the early 1990s, suffering a dire economy and riding the tide of post-cold war global democratization, the Congo made a peaceful transition from thirty years as a Marxist-Leninist single-party state to a multi-party democracy. The peace was short-lived; groups opposing elected president Pascal Lissouba mounted campaigns that by 1993 erupted in violence and established a pattern of militia-based partisan conflict that twice more climaxed in broad-scale civil war.

Violence exploded from June to October 1997, when an armed militia supporting former single-party president Sassou-Nguesso battled with forces respectively representing the interests of Lissouba and former prime minister Bernard Kolelas. Sassou's Angolan-aided forces overthrew Lissouba's government and forced him and Kolelas into exile. Newly established as president, Sassou quickly proclaimed his Fundamental Act, which replaced the 1992 constitution, and established a transitional council to serve as a three-year interim parliament. Violence again escalated, and in December 1998 rebels launched an offensive on the capital, Brazzaville, looting and burning much of the southern part of the city and displacing an estimated 250,000 Congolese. In early 1999 militia-based incursions continued throughout regions south of Brazzaville, further displacing an estimated 500,000.[1]

In his press for peace, Sassou announced in August 1999 an amnesty for surrendering militia combatants. In November an initial cease-fire agreement was signed, followed by a more comprehensive accord in December 1999. Signers of the accord agreed to demilitarization of political parties, forfeiting of arms, and amnestied reintegration of all combatants who fought between June 1997 and December 1999. The reintegration process has resulted in outbursts of vigilante violence, and the government's security forces reportedly continue to commit smaller-scale human rights breaches, but there have been no major affronts to the peace initiative. By the end of 2000 most of the 800,000 internally displaced Congolese had returned to their homes.[2]

### Status of Women

The Congolese population, however, still suffers the effects of a decade of conflict. According to the

United Nations, poverty—estimated at 70 percent in 1997—is currently a "near-universal phenomenon" throughout the country.[3] Women and children, who were ongoing targets of the militias' civilian rampage, continue in peacetime to be at risk. Although the current constitution provides for equality of all citizens, and though the government has ratified the United Nations Convention on the Elimination of All Forms of Discrimination Against Women (CEDAW), per capita income for women stands at 54 percent of that of men.[4] Women are underrepresented in the formal sector, and in rural areas they are largely confined to small-scale farming and petty commerce. An analysis of extended food assistance beneficiaries in Brazzaville found that 70 percent were female-headed households, likely reflecting a post-war increase in single mothers.[5] Although there is a Ministry of Public Service, Administrative Reform, and Promotion of Women, only two out of twenty-five cabinet members in the national government are women, and women have virtually no representation at the local level.[6] Maternal mortality rates reportedly worsened throughout the 1990s, and in its Plan for 2001-2002, the U.N. estimated that only 2 percent of Congolese women have access to contraception.[7] Abortions, illegal except when pregnancy poses a danger to the mother, nevertheless appear to be discreetly available. According to one local clinic willing to share information anonymously, twenty abortions are performed there per day. HIV/AIDS is currently estimated to be the leading cause of death among the 19 to 45 age cohort.[8] These negative indicators make it difficult for women to recover from the war, especially in the wake of well-documented and pervasive GBV.

## Gender-based Violence

### Nature and Scope

Although rape outside of marriage is illegal in the Congo, widespread sexual violence against women and children during the Congo's three waves of conflict illustrate long-standing cultural traditions supporting the exploitation of women. The Congo is a patriarchal society in which violence against women is normative and rarely reported. There are no legal protections specific to domestic violence, and marriage and family law discriminate against women, allowing polygamy and adultery for men, but prohibiting both for women. In rural areas the traditional interpretation of dowry and inheritance laws generally restrict women's ability to divorce or otherwise live independently, and domestic conflicts are typically settled by male heads within the family or, in more extreme cases, by local male officials or chiefs. Forced sex in marriage is often considered the husband's right, a conviction exacerbated by the dowry tradition. Sexual harassment and sexual assault in the workplace and schools are also apparent problems. Although public sex solicitation is illegal, remunerated sex is not. The economic collapse during the 1990s combined with the rise in female-headed households may be contributing to the reported upsurge in informal prostitution.

### Early Programming Activities

Subsequent to the conflict of 1997, the International Rescue Committee (IRC) conducted a baseline reproductive health assessment that tentatively surmised "hundreds to thousands" of women may have been sexually violated by militia forces.[9] The assessment further concluded that health personnel were generally uncomfortable discussing GBV with their patients, cleaving to a long tradition of silence.

Following from the assessment, IRC instituted the first—and, evidently, the only—program designed to address issues of GBV in Congolese society. The program launched a Brazzaville media blitz, using street theater, songs, radio, television, billboards, posters, pamphlets, and T-shirts to sensitize the population about basic issues of sexual violence against women. All the messages—some with very explicit illustrations of violence—were approved by a Congolese project advisory board comprised of government, local NGO, church, press, and community representatives. After several months of sensitization, the IRC GBV program facilitated curriculum development (by recruiting local experts) and subsequent GBV trainings to health centers and social workers on emergency reproductive health and psychosocial response. Curricula were also created for training judiciary, police, military personnel, and psychologists.

During and following the rebel incursion into south Brazzaville, displaced populations began arriving at multiple Brazzaville-based reception centers in early 1999. The IRC GBV program, primarily in collaboration with International Federation of the Red Cross (IFRC) and Médecins Sans Frontières (MSF), provided initial support to victims, ensuring that survivors received free medical treatment and social services. Approximately two thousand women from Brazzaville came forward to acknowledge sexual victimization by militia and military forces, with close to 10 percent reporting related pregnancies.[10] Extrapolating from estimates of the numbers of survivors who never sought treatment, the U.N. has suggested that five thousand women in Brazzaville alone were victims of war-related sexual violence.[11] Cases were reported of infanticide and maternal suicide, as well as rejection by the victim's husband of the unwanted child and its mother. With financial support and staffing from international organizations, some twenty-five local NGOs, hospitals, and health programs were equipped to provide basic GBV counseling and medical management.

During 1999 GBV programming existed exclusively in the Brazzaville region. As refugees began returning to Congo's southern cities in 2000, IRC staff were positioned in Dolise, the capital city of the Niari region (one of the most affected by the civil war of 1998-1999). Again, IRC's program was the first and only in the Niari region to explicitly address sexual violence. The GBV team conducted similar sensitization as that launched in Brazzaville (though on a smaller scale) and established free medical and psychosocial programs for rape survivors. IRC also moved further inside the bush to Makabana, where they trained medical providers to conduct rape exams and provide IRC-supplied medication. By mid-2001, IRC had identified close to five hundred survivors, three hundred of whom were assisted in IRC-facilitated health centers. During this period, IRC also retained a Brazzaville lawyer to examine existing legislation affecting survivors of violence in order to increase capacity for legal advocacy regarding GBV. Most recently, IRC's GBV operations have been initiated in the Loukoulela and Betou regions of northern Congo, where the United Nations High Commissioner for Refugees (UNHCR) has established services for an influx of refugees from DRC.

## Current GBV-related Programming

War disrupts absolutely, and in the case of IRC's Brazzaville GBV program, the 1998-1999 conflict had an impact on the vision and execution of the project. Although IRC had anticipated transferring the program into a two-and-one-half-year United Nations Development Program (UNDP) "Integration of Women in Development" project, funding was stalled in early 1999 because of the new fighting. The GBV program has since been operating mostly according to emergency needs. In 1998 and early 1999 NGO and donor interest in issues of war-related sexual assault was relatively strong, with organizations such as the United Nations Children's Fund (UNICEF) and the United Nations Population Fund (UNFPA) proposing complementary projects with GBV components, but in late 1999 MSF's international denouncement of the Brazzaville rapes received little attention from the international community.[12] Donor enthusiasm has since waned, perhaps because of increased attention afforded the conflict in neighboring DRC. Even so, the ongoing efforts of IRC, IFRC, and MSF, in collaboration with local programs, have succeeded in significantly changing the landscape of medical response to survivors of GBV, to the extent that the Ministry of Health's national plan of action now includes a component on sexual violence and rape during war.

### Brazzaville

IRC's GBV program substantially reduced its activities in Brazzaville when it moved its efforts to Dolise in early 2000. The several local NGOs that had developed community education and response protocols on violence are currently operating with limited to no international funding and locally based GBV sensitization activities appear to have languished. For example, the local advocacy and direct service NGO, Thomas Sankara Association, continues to provide brief counseling and medical referral for victims, but does so primarily with volunteers and funds collected from association dues. A prominent Brazzaville theater group, originally supported by IRC to develop anti-violence scenarios, similarly continues its educational street theater on a variety of topics dictated by funding incentives, but has not recently received support to conduct sensitization on GBV. Both organizations express concern that rape, domestic violence, and sexual harassment will continue to pose serious risks to Congolese women and girls in the absence of ongoing sensitization.

UNICEF, IFRC, MSF, local social workers, and an association of Congolese psychologists support or directly provide clinic and hospital-based curative services for victims of violence. Hospitals are requested to submit their sexual assault statistics to the Ministry of Health, though the Ministry's compiled statistics are not available to the public, and it is unclear how the Ministry intends to use the data. One hospital gynecologist reported seeing approximately twelve to fifteen rape cases per week—with about one-third of the rapes committed post-conflict—and at least one domestic violence case per week.

Even in the presence of ongoing violence, few initiatives are forthcoming. UNICEF plans to target the adolescent population by supporting the local Brazzaville-based NGO, ACOLVEF, to provide assistance to sexual assault survivors through counseling, training, education, and micro-enterprise opportunities. UNDP and UNFPA have recently initiated data collection on sexual violence cases in southern Congo and are also funding locally produced television broadcast videos on sexual violence against women. Both UNDP and UNFPA are interested in addressing the need for GBV-related legal reform, but have not collaborated with IRC's legal expert retained to explore the application of national and international laws on violence and women's rights. At present there appears to be little coordination among local and international agencies, and no active working groups dealing with GBV.

## Dolise

IRC's GBV activities in Dolise are similar to those developed in Brazzaville, but staff work in a more constrained environment, with limited infrastructure and material resources. When IRC entered Dolise in March 2000, the displaced community was in the first phases of return. Local government and institutions were only beginning to regroup. The IRC GBV program initially consulted with the mayor of Dolise, and with his approval created and posted a series of billboards on sexual violence. IRC also provided training for health and hospital workers on rape response protocols and established a delivery system of free gynecological examinations and basic medications to survivors. An IRC social worker currently makes home visits to identify sexual assault survivors, offering psychosocial support and medical referral, as well as support for other issues such as domestic violence. A theater group commissioned to conduct GBV sensitization has done so in Dolise's streets to wide audiences.

Local health representatives and members of Dolise's women's organizations strongly support IRC's activi-

ties, but are concerned that the limited sensitization activities and medical services are insufficient to change the culture of violence against women. In a focus group with women victims of military and militia rapes who received assistance from IRC, they expressed similar frustration with the medical care available, particularly the absence of post-natal care for babies produced from their rapes and lack of hospital services for more severe gynecological complaints, such as chronic bleeding, that surfaced after their assaults. Notably, all of these women identified themselves not only as rape survivors but also as victims of domestic violence, and all expressed fears about their HIV status. Most of the women felt stigmatized and ostracized by their community, if not their families. Other forms of violence identified by Dolise officials, health care providers, and local men and women include sexual harassment of women by bosses and teachers, incest and other forms of sexual violence against children, forced sex in marriage, ongoing coerced sex by the military, and high rates of prostitution among adolescent girls and single mothers.

## Makabana

Similar types of violence were identified by a health care provider in Makabana, whose clinic is funded by IRC. Trained by IRC to conduct free gynecological exams and provide basic medications to rape survivors, he sees patients whose predominant presenting complaints are symptoms related to sexually transmitted infections. The health care provider has also been confronted with cases of domestic violence—such as one woman whose hand was chopped off with a machete by a jealous husband—for which he has no expert resources or referrals.

Initial sensitization activities in Makabana were brief and limited to community education about the availability of free medical services to rape survivors. IRC staff judged that the military presence in Makabana and unresolved political hostilities resulted in a potentially incendiary environment not yet stable enough to examine issues of GBV.

## Summary

GBV activities initiated by the IRC program and taken up by other international and local organizations have had a marked impact in the Congo:

sensitization and training have led to medical and psychosocial services that were previously non-existent and have resulted in rape survivors seeking assistance. Standardized health protocols utilized by Brazzaville hospitals have facilitated the collection of prevalence data, which has in turn contributed to advocacy efforts. Concern about GBV has been stimulated in government and local organizations, and sexual violence is on the national health agenda. Most recently, IRC has taken on the additional task of analyzing local and international legal texts on violence against women—a critical area of investigation, given that survivor retribution for war-related rape is at risk because the government's amnesty program may provide blanket immunity for perpetrators.

The success of IRC, IFRC, MSF, and others in garnering the support of a local community previously unfamiliar with GBV prevention and response programming may be partially attributable to their ability to meet the emergent health and psychosocial needs of those traumatized by war. It is surely also attributable to participatory methods: as a matter of course, IRC first approached community representatives to engage their support for GBV activities, and consistently used local experts to develop and conduct sensitization and training activities. Another component to their successful strategy was the provision of free health services—in both Brazzaville and Dolise it was widely announced that survivors of rape could receive free services at select health clinics and hospitals. (Potential lack of confidentiality was reduced by ensuring that multiple services were offered at the clinics.) However, the general focus on short-term, emergency-oriented GBV activities has thus far limited the Congo's ability to lay a strong foundation for ongoing GBV programming, particularly outside the health sector.

Although the GBV services currently provided are critical, they are neither comprehensive nor sufficiently long term to have an impact on other forms of GBV, such as domestic violence, spousal rape, and harmful traditional practices, or on the basic attitudes that inform all types of GBV. In one telling theater campaign against sexual violence, condom distribution was discontinued because male participants reportedly associated the condoms with the necessity to protect themselves while committing rape.

Sustained programming currently exists in the form of curative rather than preventive activities. Furthermore, hospitals and health clinics have protocols and financing to provide treatment for rape, but they have not had similarly comprehensive training to respond to domestic or other forms of violence. Local NGOs experienced in GBV sensitization activities have received inconsistent support and do not have the resources to continue to expand their outreach. Brazzaville-based security forces, including police and military, participated in IRC trainings, but there appears to have been little follow-up or monitoring of GBV-related protection protocols; in fact, the military's resistance to GBV sensitization precluded further training. Similarly, judges and lawyers have received basic sensitization, but the current judicial process remains reliant on customary procedures that undermine the victim's ability to seek prosecution, such as the general requirement that victims must pay in order to retain a lawyer and process a complaint. There are few corollary support programs —income generation, social support, etc.—for women reporting violence, and local women's organizations in both Brazzaville and the Dolise area have not organized themselves around combating ongoing violence, especially in the context of larger human rights issues such as gender equity and equality.

## Recommendations

1.  If the Congo is to combat GBV, government, international, and local institutions should be catalyzed to coordinate their GBV-related activities so that prevention and response evolve to embrace issues of GBV beyond sexual violence, such as domestic violence and coerced or forced prostitution. Success in future programming will be directly related to the extent that government and donor institutions shift from remedial to forward-looking and comprehensive strategies to prevent GBV. An inter-agency working group should be established that includes representatives of the national government, international U.N. bodies, international and local NGOs.

2.  UNDP and UNFPA should follow through on their stated interest to examine laws related to GBV, from which more equitable and protective legislation may be drafted. In the immediate future, the government should institute legislation that holds perpetrators of war-related sexual violence accountable for crimes committed

during the civil conflict, and the government should support federal courts to prosecute those crimes.

3. Health services for all rape survivors—not just those reporting war-related sexual assault—should be free of cost. The Ministry of Health should institute and monitor the implementation of policies requiring that designated medical doctors throughout the Congo are trained in sexual assault forensic examinations and in providing expert testimony. The Ministry of Health should assume responsibility for collecting and analyzing data on GBV from all of Congo's hospitals and health centers, rather than only those in Brazzaville.

4. Ministries for the interior, justice, and social welfare should support the systematic integration of GBV prevention and response mandates in social services and protection sectors. The ministries should be accountable for ensuring that social workers, police, lawyers, and the judiciary are well trained in laws related to GBV, as well as in response protocols, and data collection and analysis.

5. More comprehensive research initiatives should be initiated by the government to better clarify the scope of GBV, so that programming can be adapted to address issues such as domestic violence and coerced or forced prostitution.

6. Media campaigns using radio, television, and street theater should be spearheaded by the government in collaboration with appropriate U.N. institutions, including UNFPA, UNDP, and UNICEF. These campaigns should expand their current focus beyond the issue of sexual violence.

7. In order to extend the reach of their initial successes, existing Brazzaville-based organizations already experienced in GBV sensitization and service delivery should be financed to provide training in other regions of the Congo. Community development activities should be undertaken to stimulate the formation of women's organizations, and thus create a broad local GBV advocacy base, as well as a network for general empowerment initiatives.

8. Similarly, men's organizations, churches, and local government structures should be used to involve men and male community representatives in ongoing prevention efforts.

9. GBV issues, especially in terms of mutual respect, conflict management, and sexual health, should be introduced into school curricula, and teens should be recruited to advocate against violence to their age cohort. Targeting schools will be critical in addressing the culture of violence spawned by Congo's years of civil conflict.

## Notes

1 United Nations, *U.N. Plan: Republic of Congo, 2001-2002* (Brazzaville, 2001), 4.

2 U.S. Department of State, *Country Reports on Human Rights Practices, 2000: Republic of Congo* (Washington, D.C., 2001), 1.

3 U.N., *Plan: Republic of Congo, 2001-2002*, 3.

4 U.N., *Plan: Republic of Congo, 2001-2002*, 20.

5 U.N., *Plan: Republic of Congo, 2001-2002*, 11.

6 U.N., *Plan: Republic of Congo, 2001-2002*, 22.

7 U.N., *Plan: Republic of Congo, 2001-2002*, 28.

8 U.N., *Plan: Republic of Congo, 2001-2002*, 28.

9 International Rescue Committee (IRC), *Addressing Emergency Reproductive Health Needs: Pilot Minimum Initial Service Package Project Report* (Brazzaville, 1998), 1.

10 IRC, *Gender-based Violence Program in Republic of Congo Project Report* (Brazzaville, 2000), 3.

11 U.N., *Plan: Republic of Congo, 2001-2002*, 18.

12 L. Shanks, N. Ford, M. Schull, and K. de Jong, "Responding to Rape," *The Lancet* 357, no. 9252 (January 2001): 304.

# Post-genocide Situation in *Rwanda*

February 18-28, 2001

## Background

### Historical Context

In 1994 Rwanda distinguished itself in the annals of world history by concluding a one hundred-day genocide during which militia groups worked in methodical concert with the ruling Hutu government's Forces Armées Rwandaises (FAR) to hack, rape, burn, and otherwise brutalize to death an estimated 750,000 Rwandan Tutsi and Hutu moderates. The searingly efficient success of the genocide was in part the result of an unresponsive international community; it was also the realization of a well-orchestrated, government-supported fomentation of ethnic hatred between the Rwandan Hutu majority and their minority Tutsi colleagues, neighbors, and relatives.[1]

Whether or not the Hutu-Tutsi divide that precipitated the genocide can be legitimately expressed in terms of ethnic difference—an issue of debate among historians—it does seem clear that the colonization of Rwanda exacerbated class distinctions among the Tutsi elite and the Hutu populace. The Belgians, for example, issued ID cards for Tutsi and Hutu based on the numbers of cows they had, thus solidifying a previously porous social structure. During Rwanda's post-World War II transition from colonial rule to independence, the Hutu launched a rebellion against the Tutsi monarchy. The related 1959 massacre of Tutsi was for the Hutu a socialist victory; for the Tutsi it was the "beginning of ethnic fratricide" that resulted in the first mass exodus of Tutsi refugees to neighboring countries.[2]

Hutu rule, including discriminatory practices against Tutsi, remained largely uncontested for the next thirty years. In the early 1990s the increasingly empowered and aggressive rebel army Rwandese Patriotic Front (RPF), comprised mostly of exiled Tutsi advocating for Tutsi repatriation and democratic government, laid claim through a series of armed offenses to territories in northern Rwanda, displacing some one million Hutu. Although Hutu President Habyarimana formally acceded to opposition requests for democracy by signing the Arusha Accords in 1993, his government continued to foster ethnic hatred and instill fears of a return to Tutsi hegemony. Habyarimana's assassination in April 1994 (allegedly by Hutu government radicals) was seemingly the call to action required by Hutu extremists to launch their Tutsi and moderate Hutu extermination campaign.[3]

The RPF advanced on Rwanda's capital city of Kigali in July 1994, definitively defeating the FAR and the militias, and clearing the way for an RPF-dominated "Government of National Unity." Fearing retribution, Hutu genocide leaders, as well as hundreds of thousands of other Hutu, fled to neighboring countries, crossing borders in advance of a tide of exiled Tutsi making their return to Rwanda. In 1996 many Hutu refugees, who had managed for several years to survive disease, militia control, and host government hostility in highly unstable refugee camps, opted or were forced to repatriate, so that by the late 1990s post-genocide Rwanda had evolved into a society of collective traumas.[4]

The genocide exacted a heavy toll on families and communities and also destroyed the country's economic, social, and political infrastructure. Thousands of genocide suspects have been summarily arrested, even absent a formal charge; some of the more than 100,000 currently awaiting trial have been detained since 1994.[5] In spite of the relatively high level of international aid per capita following the genocide, the numbers of returnees and shifting population movements, as well as repeated Hutu-based insurgencies in Rwanda's northwest region, considerably slowed the country's ability to move from emergency to development.[6] Although social and economic initiatives are gaining ground, an estimated 70 percent of the population lives in poverty, and 90 percent are engaged in subsistence agriculture.[7]

## Status of Women

Surviving women and children remain among the most affected; in some communities widows make up 60 percent of heads of households.[8] Despite recent notable gains in the numbers of women in key government positions, women are still underrepresented in the ranks of power, both within the government and in civil society posts.[9] A post-genocide proliferation of local NGOs providing education, social, and financial assistance to women have in some measure redressed this void.[10] Their work has been strengthened and reinforced by the advocacy efforts and support of the relatively new Ministry for Gender and Women in Development (MIGEPROFE). The international community has also had a key role in supporting women and their organizations, most notably through the United Nations Development Program's (UNDP) Trust Fund for Women; the U.S. Agency for International Development's (USAID) Women in Development Program; and the United Nations High Commissioner for Refugees' (UNHCR) Rwanda Women's Initiative (RWI). In terms of genocide-related violence, the RWI in particular provided direct funding to local women's programs providing psychosocial assistance. Several of these local NGOs, as well as MIGEPROFE and a few international NGOs, have led efforts to address the effects of GBV perpetrated during the genocide.

## Gender-based Violence

### During the Genocide

In a glaring conflation of gender and ethnic biases, the first three of the Hutu "Ten Commandments," which reportedly circulated widely before the genocide, exhort Hutu men to avoid the seduction of Tutsi women, and accord favor to Hutu women, who are "more dignified and more conscientious in their roles as woman, wife, and mother" than their Tutsi counterparts, and "pretty, good secretaries, and more honest."[11] Such propaganda illustrates and reinforces some of the gender issues at play in the atrocities committed by both male and female *genocidaires*: by specifically raising the specter of Tutsi women's enticing sexuality, the commandments simultaneously promote and devalue the Tutsi woman in terms of her sexuality, laying the groundwork for violence that targeted that image. Although exact numbers of victims are unknown, it is estimated that a quarter- to a half-million women and girls of all ages *survived* rape. (The figures, loosely extrapolated from the estimates of the two to five thousand babies reportedly born of genocide sexual violence, assume a 1 to 4 percent chance of pregnancy with every sexual encounter.[12]) It is impossible to account for the numbers of women who were raped and then murdered. In a 1999 research initiative undertaken by the local Rwandan NGO Association of Widows of the Genocide (Avega), 39 percent of women interviewed acknowledged being raped, and 74 percent stated they knew women who were raped. Given the cultural stigma associated with rape and the subsequent isolation of victims—a stunningly low 6 percent of women interviewed had sought medical care since the genocide—it is likely that the actual number of rape survivors lies somewhere between these percentages. Avega's findings of types of genocidal sexual violence reinforce earlier findings of human rights investigators: atrocities included sexual slavery, gang rape, forced incest, purposeful HIV transmission and impregnation, and genital mutilation.[13]

### Beyond the Genocide

According to the Avega report, GBV is not a new phenomenon in Rwanda. "Violence in everyday life is deeply rooted in the memory and habits" of the Rwandese, finding its expression in traditions such as the dowry, polygamy (illegal but condoned), forced marriage (illegal but prosecutable only by the victim's family, who may often be complicit), and forced sex in marriage.[14] The genocide, directly and indirectly, further engendered violence against women and girls. For example, Hutu refugees were exposed to sexual violence in their camps in Tanzania and Zaire.[15]

Domestic violence—claimed in a Rwandan proverb to be a necessary precursor to achieving woman-hood—was estimated at 20 percent in the 1995 Rwandan National Report to the Beijing Fourth World Conference on Women.[16] Women's represen-tatives believe that this number is low and that, in any case, domestic violence increased in the geno-cide's trail of tension and despair. Prostitution, though officially illegal, has reportedly risen dramatically. Even more alarmingly, in a nationwide government survey of prostitutes, 76 percent of those interviewed who had undergone HIV testing were seropositive.[17] A spate of rapes of young children by adult males was also a post-genocide phenomenon, attributed on the one hand to misperceptions that having sex with young children cured HIV/AIDS, and on the other hand to the "near impunity enjoyed by those people responsible for violence during the genocide."[18]

Impunity has been a feature of rape-related genocide crimes, in part because the judicial response has been extremely slow. The success of international and Rwandan women's advocates in obtaining a "category 1" classification (punishable by death) for genocidal rapes involving "sexual torture" has heightened public awareness of the severity of rape, which was previ-ously categorized as a misdemeanor, traditionally requiring reparations provided by the perpetrator to the victim's family. Yet few convictions have been levied by the International Criminal Tribunal for Rwanda, and women's organizations have complained that lack of security and confidentiality for survivors has discouraged them from speaking with tribunal investigators about their assaults.[19] The traditional *gacaca* system of community-based courts, reformulat-ed by the Rwandan government as a way to expedite the thousands of accused awaiting trial for genocide crimes, will when implemented exclude category 1 offenses and thus further limit the prosecution of genocidal rapists.

However, several post-genocide rape cases have received judicial attention—due in large part to the advocacy of MIGEPROFE and local human rights and women's organizations. Some recent cases are reportedly being prosecuted to the full extent of

existing laws, with punishments ranging from five to twenty years.[20] The Ministry of Justice (MINIJUST) has also facilitated short sensitization trainings on violence against women to the newly installed and overwhelmingly male national police force, but women's representatives suggest that police response to rape victims is still inconsistent and reflective of long-standing gender discriminatory practices. Response to most other non-genocide crimes against women, such as domestic violence, generally remains the domain of the family and the community; they have not yet achieved the same nationwide attention as rape.

## Current GBV-related Programming

Compared to resources that flooded Rwanda after the genocide, the contributions of the international community to address genocide-related sexual assault were limited and belated. In her report following a visit to Rwanda in 1998, the United Nations Special Rapporteur on Violence Against Women expressed concern "at the incomprehensible absence of any pro-grams supporting women victims of violence by any United Nations agencies and operations present in Rwanda."[21] A notable exception to this absence was the World Health Organization's (WHO) project to address the health needs of women and girls who survived violence. WHO's initiative began in 1997 with national education campaigns and continued until 1999 to provide medical supplies and basic psy-chosocial training to health care and social service providers.[22] Even so, WHO's brief trainings were admittedly introductory, and funding is not yet secured to implement the evaluation phase of their project. RWI also has GBV as one component of its mandate, yet only a few of the RWI-funded women's organizations have targeted issues related to violence against women. Plagued by dramatic shifts in fund-ing, RWI has not been sufficiently consistent and/or strategic in its outreach to rural women affected by the genocide, thus limiting its overall "empowerment" objective.[23] In fact, all of RWI implementing partners are Kigali-based.[24]

More recently, several United Nations agencies, in-cluding UNDP, the United Nations Population Fund (UNFPA), and the United Nations Development Fund for Women (UNIFEM), have undertaken efforts to address GBV. With support from UNIFEM, for example, the Minister for Gender participated in a

1999 global videoconference on violence against women, and on International Women's Day in March 2000 MIGEPROFE initiated a year-long media campaign to Stop Violence Against Women and the Girl Child. The Minister for Gender continues to be a staunch proponent of the importance of addressing GBV, and has worked together with the Ministry of Health (MINISANTE) on HIV/AIDS and prostitution, with MINIJUST on GBV prosecution issues, and with the Ministry of Social Affairs on providing social assistance to victims of genocide-related sexual violence. MINISANTE has included sexual violence as a component of its national reproductive health policy, but protocols for response have not been standardized or implemented.

MIGEPROFE's Secretariat for Women's Organizations has been charged with coordinating the large numbers of women's NGOs and emerging government-supported local women's councils in order to enlarge the capacity to prevent and respond systematically to GBV countrywide. The Secretariat's effort will be considerably enhanced by UNIFEM's current national mapping project of all women's NGOs. At the moment, however, no consolidated umbrella project exists for GBV. Most direct services to GBV victims are the purview of a small number of Kigali-based women's NGOs, whose financial and technical support comes from a similarly small number of international donors and NGOs, and whose field outreach is limited by their lack of funding and administrative capacity.

Kigali

Pro-Femmes/Twese Hamwe is the Kigali-based umbrella organization for local women's NGOs; it has grown from thirteen to thirty-eight organizations since its 1994 inception. In spite of its size, the umbrella does not yet serve a coordinating function, particularly with regard to GBV programming. Of participating NGOs, six have developed the capacity to provide services to survivors of GBV. Among them is Haguruka, a legal advocacy NGO whose 330 paralegals, working nationwide, accompany rape victims to doctors and police, provide legal counsel, and attempt to facilitate the prosecutory process. Last year Haguruka also received over 1,500 domestic violence complaints, though women rarely sought prosecution of their husbands because of economic constraints, social stigma, and fear of family and partner retribution. A model former employee

of Haguruka now works as a consultant to several women's organizations to conduct field-based advocacy efforts, most notably convincing the police and judiciary to attend to GBV cases. Another Pro-Femmes member active in GBV response is Avega. In addition to their research initiative on genocide violence mentioned above, Avega provides rape survivor counseling to widows of the genocide.

Avega and three other women's organizations providing GBV counseling and case management services—Barakabaho, Icyuzuzo, and Clinique de L'espoir—are currently receiving assistance from Médecins Sans Frontières (MSF) to further improve their clinical capacities to respond to survivors and to develop an inter-agency clinical supervisory and support network. MSF's capacity-building project will enhance the earlier efforts of the Irish NGO Trocaire. Although Trocaire's commitment to long-term counselor training of select members of these NGOs was a positive departure from the more usual short-term trauma training models that overwhelmed Rwanda following the genocide, Trocaire's objectives did not include, as do MSF's, oversight and assistance with administration and coordination of counseling services among local women's NGOs.

Another reputable and long-standing Kigali organization working with female survivors of the genocide is the Polyclinic of Hope. Started by Church World Service in 1995, the Polyclinic is now operating under the umbrella of the local Rwanda Women's Network. Polyclinic services to over five hundred registered members include free medical care, psychosocial counseling and support activities, income generation support, and shelter assistance. The Rwanda Women's Network's overall orientation toward women's empowerment informs the strategies of Polyclinic, so that women are encouraged to develop community networks of mutual assistance and support. Like most local NGOs, Polyclinic is continually confronted with challenges of obtaining ongoing funding. In order to ensure that their model program continues, they are considering joining with MINISANTE to replicate their services within hospitals nationwide.

As yet, MINISANTE has no national program to address GBV. Select hospitals have social workers and health care providers trained in trauma counseling by WHO and the Trocaire-supported organization Association Rwandaise des Conseillers en

Traumatisme (ARCT). With rare exceptions rape victims continue to be required to pay for forensic exams, for which there are no special protocols or specially trained doctors available. Association Rwandaise Pour le Bien-Etre Familial (ARBEF), the long-standing local arm of the International Planned Parenthood Federation, also has no specific services targeting victims. When a survivor requests rape treatment, ARBEF will provide reduced-fee medical treatment for sexually transmitted infections as well as general emotional support. ARBEF workers acknowledge they are not trained to provide counseling for GBV. They have instead tried to adapt their methods of HIV/AIDS counseling, "telling her to avoid such conditions so as not to be raped again." Although formal records of domestic violence reports are not kept, the clinical director of ARBEF reported that large numbers of clients reveal histories of domestic violence.

## Byumba Refugee Camp

This camp in northern Rwanda is one of three in Rwanda serving Congolese and Burundian refugees. The American Refugee Committee (ARC), alarmed by reports of domestic violence, forced marriage, and sexual violence against Congolese women within the Byumba camp, facilitated a community education series on violence prevention and response. Although the sensitization was short term, representatives of the camp committee feel that the trainings significantly reduced incidents of violence, particularly the high rates of forced marriage. Even without methods for measuring the impact of the program, the camp representatives credited the sensitization's "success" to the involvement of MIGEPROFE, the local government, and UNHCR in educating the camp population that rape and forced marriage are illegal and ensuring that reported cases were brought to trial. Representatives of the camp committee also attributed the sensitization's success to the broad-based community education approach: teachers instructed children; representatives of each of the seventy-two camp sections educated their section leaders; and health care providers educated patients.

In spite of the reported achievements of the project, several Byumba camp representatives alluded to ongoing problems, such as coerced sex and prostitution of young girls outside the camp, and ongoing though less frequent incidents of domestic violence within the camps. A UNHCR protection representa-tive paints a much more sober picture; she feels that non-reporting of many types of violence remains commonplace. In an example of the perils of reporting, one camp community ostracized a sixteen-year-old impregnated by a well-liked camp leader after she identified her rapist to UNHRC. At the behest of the community, UNHCR released the leader back to his camp after a brief detention. It is impossible to determine the current rates of refugee violence, as there are no ongoing prevention or response programs specifically addressing GBV within the camps.

## Summary

More than seven years have passed since Rwanda's genocide, and yet most existing GBV programs have not advanced beyond addressing the victimizations perpetrated during the genocide. This lack of progress reflects the profound destruction brought about by those few months in 1994. It also reflects the failure of the international community to respond to the issue of genocide-related GBV efficiently and effectively. Until the last two years, almost all GBV initiatives were delivered at the local level, primarily in Kigali, with the assistance of international NGOs operating largely independent of one another. Furthermore, all of the NGOs providing services have GBV as only one component of usually extensive programming, a probable response to the donor-driven necessity to diversify services in order to obtain sufficient operational funds. The need to generalize organizational mandates has undermined NGOs' abilities to evolve specialized, comprehensive, or in-depth skills in the area of GBV.

Certainly the environmental challenges to the international and local organizations cannot be underestimated. In the early post-genocide period, national government was overwhelmed, civil sector organizations were extremely weak, and ongoing conflict and population movements complicated efforts to coordinate and strengthen community-based initiatives. Even so, early post-genocide GBV programming in Rwanda may provide a case study for the outcomes of humanitarian projects that are primarily curative with limited or no preventive components, that are small in scale, and that do not place conflict-related violence in the broader context of gender inequities. The results appear to be that post-conflict violence has escalated, and that few women are seeking and few organizations are offering assistance for GBV outside the realm of sexual assault.

Nevertheless, promising shifts have taken place in Rwanda within the last two years that may change the landscape of future efforts to address GBV. Most importantly, MIGEPROFE and the Secretariat for Women's Organizations are vocal advocates for confronting violence against women. All Ministries—notably Gender, Justice, Social Affairs and Health—appear to be committed to coordinating with each other regarding GBV, as well as to coordinating the activities of NGOs. MINIJUST has shown a commitment to expediting judicial response to rape cases. MINISANTE has similarly embraced the importance of addressing GBV by including it within their national reproductive health policy, though implementation of the policy has not been initiated. The relatively new locally based and nationally supported women's councils may, with technical assistance, be a resource for facilitating coordination of GBV prevention and response activities, especially if they are not viewed competitively by local women's NGOs as attempting to usurp precarious NGO funding. The success of local NGOs in providing services, even in the face of challenges such as short-term funding, limited technical assistance, and administrative inexperience, is a testament to the capacity and commitment of Rwandan women, and it speaks to the potential that women's organizations offer in the reconstruction of the country's social infrastructure.

## Recommendations

1.  International donors must consider prevention of GBV an integral activity of long-term development and fund accordingly. Models of short-term, curative services funded during the emergency phase are no longer suitable to the society's needs. Priority should be given to supporting the government's institutionalization of GBV prevention and response activities through the design and implementation of GBV-related policy, as well as through support to government and civil sector actors at the national and local levels. In order to facilitate this, local NGOs with experience in GBV must be financially and technically assisted to provide training and consultation.

2.  An interagency working group should be established, led by MIGEPROFE, including representatives of relevant ministries, U.N. bodies, and international and local NGOS. The interagency working group should monitor the progressive efforts by the national and local governments to institute prevention and response activities.

3.  MIGEPROFE should be fully supported with technical assistance and funding by international donors and the Rwandan government to continue its ongoing efforts to address GBV. The Ministry must receive particular assistance in developing the skills and mandate of locally based women's councils, so that the councils can serve their communities by enhancing existing NGO accessibility and coordination. The Ministry should also receive assistance necessary to coordinate the activities of the NGOs so that they may work cooperatively toward common goals rather than exclusively and competitively. The Ministry's proven success in changing discriminatory inheritance laws against women should be utilized in addressing laws related to violence against women and girls. MIGEPROFE should also ensure that all other ministries have policies relevant to GBV.

4.  MINSANTE should require that their implementing partners institute supportive protocols to respond to women seeking medical exams for sexual and physical assault. Women should be encouraged to pursue treatment through broad-based media campaigns and through the provision of free services for providers. Model NGOs already experienced in the provision of health services to survivors, such as the Polyclinic of Hope, should be consulted for program design, and accessed for trainers and service providers. MINISANTE should endorse Polyclinic's proposal to create centers within hospitals where women can access services similar to those currently provided by the Polyclinic's Kigali-based center. Data should be collected at all health centers and submitted to MINISANTE for regular monitoring and evaluation of health response mechanisms.

5.  MINIJUST should provide important advocacy regarding the necessity for police forces and judiciary to respond appropriately to cases of GBV.

MINIJUST should continue to facilitate trainings for police officers and create specialized units in the police forces to monitor cases and maintain data systems on case reports, with the requirement that data be regularly submitted for review by MINIJUST. Efforts should be made to recruit more women into the police forces. MINIJUST should also ensure that the judiciary receives ongoing education about laws affecting GBV survivors, so that cases are tried according to statutory rather than customary law.

6. International NGOs should create GBV programs in close collaboration with local initiatives, with the goal of strengthening established programs through capacity building and technical assistance. Such collaboration will require a respect for NGOs' existing management structures and commitment to long-term yet flexible support.

7. Local NGOs addressing GBV should incorporate preventive activities in all areas of programming, with particular attention to empowering women and girls through community organizing and self-help programming. Increased specialization in GBV prevention and response will surely lead to expanded services addressing a spectrum of survivor needs, such as psychosocial centers, women's resource centers, safe houses, and increased community outreach and involvement. Local NGOs should also recognize the benefits of collaboration with other NGOs through their Pro-Femmes umbrella, women's councils, and MIGEPROFE. The successful advocacy activities of Pro-Femmes members illustrate the potential impact of cooperation among NGOs, especially if Pro-Femmes can further develop its coordination, networking, and fundraising strategies.

8. Men, who are notably absent from GBV initiatives, should be encouraged to offer their support and expertise in addressing gender violence, and should also be considered as potential service recipients.

## Notes

1   P. Gourevitch, *We Wish to Inform You That Tomorrow We Will Be Killed With Our Families: Stories from Rwanda* (New York, 1998).

2   United Nations, Special Rapporteur on Violence Against Women, *Report of the Mission to Rwanda on the Issues of Violence Against Women in Situations of Armed Conflict* (Geneva, 1998), Addendum 1, 4.

3   C. Newbury and H. Baldwin, *Aftermath: Women in Post-genocide Rwanda*, US Agency for International Development Working Paper 303 (Washington, D.C., 2000), 2.

4   Newbury and Baldwin, *Aftermath*, 2.

5   U. S. Department of State, *Country Reports on Human Rights Practices, 2000: Rwanda*, Bureau of Democracy, Human Rights, and Labor (Washington, D.C., 2001), 5.

6   U.N., *Profile of United Nations Programs 1998-2000, U.N. Rwanda Issues Paper* (Geneva, 2000), 6.

7   U.S. Department of State, *Country Reports on Human Rights Practices, 2000: Rwanda*, 1.

8   Newbury and Baldwin, *Aftermath*, 7.

9   Women's Commission for Refugee Women and Children, *Rebuilding Rwanda: A Struggle Men Cannot Do Alone* (New York, 2000), 3.

10  Newbury and Baldwin, *Aftermath*, 2.

11  H. Hamilton, "Rwanda's Women: The Key to Reconstruction," *Journal of Humanitarian Assistance* (January 2000): 2.

12  S. Swiss, "Rape as a Crime of War," *Journal of the American Medical Association* 270, No. 5 (August 1993): 613.

13  Association of Widows of the Genocide (Avega), *Survey on Violence Against Women in Rwanda, Avega Agahozo* (Kigali, 1999), 23-24.

14  Human Rights Watch, *Shattered Lives: Sexual Violence during the Rwandan Genocide and Its Aftermath* (New York, 1996), 20.

15  Hamilton, "Rwanda's Women," 4.

16  Human Rights Watch, *Shattered Lives*, 20.

17  Rwanda Ministry of Gender, Family, and Social Affairs, *Study on Prostitution and AIDS in Rwanda* (Kigali, 1998), 3.

18  Avega, "Survey on Violence Against Women in Rwanda," 37.

19  Human Rights Watch, *Human Rights Watch World Report 2001* (New York, 2001), 457.

20  U.S. Department of State, *Country Reports on Human Rights Practices, 2000: Rwanda*, 9.

21  U.N., Special Rapporteur on Violence Against Women, *Report of the Mission to Rwanda*, 19.

22  World Health Organization, *Amagara Yacu: Our Health* (Geneva, 2000), 3.

23  Women's Commission for Refugee Women and Children, *You Cannot Dance If You Cannot Stand: A Review of the Rwanda Women's Initiative and the United Nations High Commissioner for Refugees' Commitment to Gender Equality in Post-Conflict Settings* (New York, 2001), 1-2.

24  Women's Commission, *You Cannot Dance If You Cannot Stand*, 18.

# Internally Displaced in
# *Sierra Leone*

February 5-15, 2001

## Background

### Historical Context

Since gaining independence from British rule in 1961, resource-rich Sierra Leone has been characterized by economic exploitation, public unrest, and political instability. During its first thirty years of self-rule, a series of governments, often established by way of coups rather than elections, was unsuccessful in containing the growing discontent and divisiveness of Sierra Leone's ethnic and political factions. By the early 1990s the Revolutionary United Front (RUF) manifested a powerful rebel alliance with neighboring Liberia and succeeded, after five years of devastating civil war, to wrest control of much of Sierra Leone's diamond producing regions. The RUF's trademark mutilation, as well as forced induction, abduction, rape, and execution of civilians, also succeeded in terrorizing and dislocating over half of the country's five million inhabitants. Many civilians crossed the border into Guinea and Liberia, and others fled to Sierra Leone's capital city of Freetown or were otherwise internally displaced.

The promising multiparty elections in 1996 that popularly voted Ahmad Tejan Kabbah and his Sierra Leone People's Party into power resulted in a short-lived peace agreement with the RUF. In the face of resumed RUF hostilities, Kabbah fatefully designated a Civil Defense Force (CDF) to assist the Sierra Leone Army (SLA) in defeating the RUF. Breakaway leaders of SLA responded to this insult by staging a coup, driving Kabbah into exile, establishing a junta

with RUF, and inciting looting and a murderous rampage in Freetown. In 1998 the Economic Organization of West African States Monitoring Group (ECOMOG) deployed Nigerian forces to drive the junta out of Freetown and restore Kabbah to power. The RUF leader, Foday Sankoh, was jailed and sentenced to death, thus instigating a January 1999 rebel advance on Freetown that resulted in the further maiming, rape, and murder of thousands of civilians and the eventual release of Sankoh to United Nations monitors.

The heralded July 1999 Lomé Peace Accords included in its Disarmament, Demobilization, and Reintegration (DDR) plan a power-sharing agreement between RUF and the Kabbah government, notably designating Sankoh as chairman of the government commission responsible for diamond mining. The U.N. Security Council then introduced a peacekeeping force, the U.N. Mission in Sierra Leone (UNAMSIL), and by April 2000 ECOMOG troops were withdrawn and humanitarian organizations established or reestablished basic relief programs in areas occupied by RUF. A National Commission for Reconstruction, Resettlement, and Rehabilitation (NCRRR) was created to coordinate assistance to the internally displaced (IDPs), returning refugees, and ex-combatants. Even so, rebel violence sparked by Sankoh and led by RUF and the Westside Boys, an ex-SLA faction, once again flared—targeting civilians, UNAMSIL, and humanitarian workers, and further increasing the ranks of IDPs. The Lomé Accords' power-sharing agreement collapsed, Sankoh was once again detained, and the RUF resumed exclusive and hostile control of its diamond fiefdoms. SLA and CDF militia rearmed, humanitarian workers were evacuated from rebel territories, and the government of Sierra Leone launched military attacks in RUF locations using helicopter gunships. Meanwhile, regional tensions escalated along the Guinean and Liberian borders, such that by early 2001 Sierra Leone's internal crises were further exacerbated by a swell of repatriating refugees unable to return to their homes in eastern and northern provinces.

## Current Situation

At present, the cease-fire brokered by Kabbah in late 2000 remains tentative and rebel forces continue an only slightly mitigated reign of terror. Nevertheless, the U.N.-assisted government is moving forward in regions not held by RUF with its DDR plan, and the NCRRR is similarly advancing disarmament incentives. Humanitarian aid agencies are operating in about half the country, trying to address some of the effects of Sierra Leone's protracted conflict. Their task overwhelms, given that Sierra Leone is at the bottom of the Human Development Index: life expectancy—at thirty-seven years in 2000—continues to decline; child and maternal mortality rates are at record international highs; per capita income stands at about $150 per year.[1] Malaria, pneumonia, tuberculosis, bloody diarrhea, and HIV/AIDS are common,[2] and severe food shortages are resulting in an estimated one hundred starvation deaths per day.[3] Against this alarming backdrop of social ills, women and girls continue to suffer the additional spectrum of violent gender-based abuses and their consequences.

## Gender-based Violence

### During Conflict

Throughout Sierra Leone's ten-year war, the RUF systematically used the bodies of civilian women and girls to advance their brutal agenda of terrorizing, demoralizing, and destroying communities. In a comprehensive prevalence survey of 991 IDP women and their family members conducted by Physicians for Human Rights (PHR) in 2001, almost all households (94 percent) reported some exposure to war-related violence and 13 percent reported incidents of war-related sexual assault. Extrapolating from their findings, PHR estimates that approximately 50,000 to 64,000 IDP women may have histories of war-related

assault.[4] Médecins Sans Frontières (MSF), in collaboration with the local NGO Forum for Women Educationalists (FAWE), treated approximately two thousand women victims of rapes that occurred in and around Freetown during the January 1999 rebel incursion, and another two thousand victims, mostly IDPs, living in camps in the Bo and Kenema regions. Some survivors had severe gynecological problems, the majority had sexually transmitted diseases, and at least ten percent were pregnant.[5] The tradition of excising all or part of the clitoris and labia, which ceremoniously ushers an estimated 80 to 90 percent of Sierra Leonean girls into womanhood,[6] may also introduce among sexual assault survivors—particularly virgin girls—increased rates of genital trauma, HIV/AIDS, and other sexually transmitted infections.

Testimony taken by Human Rights Watch, Amnesty International, and PHR indicate that the RUF raped as a matter of course, often in gangs, often in front of family members. They forced boys and men to rape their mothers and wives. They abducted women and girls—reportedly targeting virgins—and compelled them into sexual and domestic slavery. They mutilated women's genitals with knives, burning wood, and gun barrels. They sexually assaulted and then disemboweled pregnant women. They rounded up girls and repeatedly raped and then abandoned them. And in the 1999 Lomé Accords they were given blanket amnesty for their abuses.[7]

The amnesty provision, which was presumably designed to facilitate reintegration, may have instead contributed to, or at the very least did not deter, further sexual abuses. In its year 2000 report, Human Rights Watch suggested that even after the signing of the Lomé Accords, a "hellish cycle of rape, sexual assault, and mutilation" of women and girls continued to be perpetrated by "all sides," including pro-government forces.[8]

### Beyond Conflict

It is perhaps not surprising that a culture that has spawned such apparently high rates of war-related sexual violence also suffers from high rates of domestic partner abuse. In a national report to the 1995 Beijing Conference on Women, violence against women was identified as a "long-standing problem."[9] More recently, cross-sectional research undertaken in Freetown in 1998 found that 66.7 percent of 144 women surveyed had been beaten by an intimate partner—of whom 60 percent required medical treatment for injuries. Of the 50.7 percent who acknowledged having been forced to have sex, boyfriends and husbands ranked in the ninetieth percentile as the perpetrators.[10] In the PHR 2001 population-based research of IDP women, more than half of those surveyed believed their husbands had the right to beat them.[11]

Prostitution is also on the rise as a result of the increased presence of international peacekeepers, as well as Sierra Leone's economic collapse and population dislocation. A 1999 national government survey of over two thousand prostitutes found that 37 percent were less than fifteen years of age; more than 80 percent were unaccompanied or displaced children; and all declared an intention to stop engaging in prostitution once alternative work became available.[12] However, the opportunity for reasonably remunerative work is slim: literacy rates among women are around 23 percent to men's 36 percent, so that women predominate in petty businesses and agriculture; in formal sector employment, women constitute only 8 percent of administrative and managerial positions.[13] This inability to escape from commercial sex work has even more dire consequences when weighed against the growing HIV crisis in Sierra Leone: a 1997 survey of Freetown prostitutes found that 70 percent were HIV-positive, as compared to 26 percent in 1995.[14]

Although Sierra Leone ratified the Convention on the Elimination of All Forms of Discrimination Against Women (CEDAW) in 1998, and the national constitution provides for equal rights for both sexes, there are few specific laws that protect women against GBV.[15] Rape is punishable by up to fourteen years' imprisonment, but domestic violence is not recognized as a crime, nor is prostitution or sex solicitation.[16] Even though the national age of consent is sixteen, girls in villages may be forced or encouraged into earlier sexual relationships or marriages, reflecting the implementation of local customary law and practice in cases where national law is not enforced. Female genital excision prevails, as does polygamy. Customary inheritance laws often discriminate against women, and women are disproportionately excluded from education, professional employment, and community leadership. Women are also underrepresented in senior government: only two of eighteen cabinet members and only seven of eighty legislators are women.[17]

## Current GBV-related Programming

In spite of Sierra Leone's evident history of gender discrimination and abuse, recent activities at the international, national, and local level show promise in addressing and improving the rights of Sierra Leonean women and girls. International human rights organizations have called for the recognition of sexual atrocities perpetrated against Sierra Leonean women as a crime against humanity, punishable by an international tribunal. The government has designed national policies on gender mainstreaming and the advancement of women that include provisions for improving protections for women against violence, and has designated the Ministry of Social Welfare, Gender, and Children's Affairs (MSWGCA) to monitor the implementation of those policies. Most significantly, efforts at the local level have resulted in increased awareness of and response to survivors of GBV.

### Freetown

Sierra Leone, or at least Freetown, has an impressive number of local NGOs. In the face of the country's violent history and extreme poverty, civil sector initiatives have surfaced as an antidote to the lack of government-supported programming. This is especially true with regard to women's issues, which have until recently been virtually absent from the national agenda. Sierra Leone's Women's Forum—organized in 1994 as an NGO coordinating body—is comprised, for example, of over forty local women's organizations variously seeking to advance the education, welfare, and general status of women and girls. Following the 1999 rebel incursion into Freetown, several of these organizations incorporated GBV prevention and response activities into their programming. A brief description of some of the more prominent initiatives is provided below. In large part, local NGOs are operating with volunteer staff and limited financial resources. Their reach and impact are directly related to the extent they are able to obtain ongoing international financing and technical support.

According to a representative of the Sierra Leone Women's Forum, supportive counseling, previously unavailable, became popular during the war. Western therapeutic models have been adapted to local traditions by including storytelling, proverbs, and singing in the treatment process. One of the most well-organized and well-supported GBV counseling programs was undertaken by FAWE, a member organization of the Women's Forum. Although FAWE's original purpose, when conceived in 1995, was to promote education among girls, the organization developed supportive programming for GBV victims following the January 1999 Freetown invasion because they perceived that GBV victims were especially vulnerable to exclusion from education as a result of their social stigmatization and related isolation, medical problems, and lack of financial resources. With support from MSF and in collaboration with MSF, MSWGCA, and the Sierra Leone Association of University Women (SLAUW), FAWE developed a team of counselors trained to provide brief counseling, case management, and referrals for free medical services to victims. They also provided micro-enterprise support and education assistance. They worked with collaborating organizations to raise awareness of their services and the availability of free medical treatment, and to conduct sensitization campaigns aimed at decreasing the social stigma of rape.

Despite success in accessing approximately two thousand victims in the first year of FAWE's Freetown project, MSF funding was short-lived (though MSF continues to invest their resources in an independent MSF-run counseling center for trauma survivors). The United Nations High Commissioner for Refugees (UNHCR) offered extension funding that allowed the program to continue for another two months, but services and staff have since been curtailed and prospects for future GBV funding are uncertain. Other organizations face similar limits: the local arm of the international NGO Christian Children's Fund, for example, had a community-based initiative to train health care workers, teachers (in collaboration with SLAUW), and community representatives on basic therapeutic responses to girl victims of violence, but did not receive ongoing funding to continue community organizing and capacity building of the six hundred trainees. The locally run and well-respected Marie Stopes Clinics likewise report a lack of financing required to expand outreach to rape victims—perhaps through mobile clinics—to areas in which there is identified need. The National Association on Violence Against Women (NAVAW) has worked through its volunteers to provide education to police on issues of violence against women, but they too have not received sufficient funds to continue their efforts or to expand their outreach beyond Freetown.

Funding issues represent one limitation in locally based GBV prevention and response. Other limitations are related to the reporting procedures for victims seeking legal recourse. The Council of Churches of Sierra Leone (CCSL)—which, like the Campaign for Good Governance and Democracy (CGG), has attempted to provide advocacy and legal support to victims—stresses that the legal process is structured so as to discourage reporting: police officers are generally not sympathetic to victims; those who have been raped must pay for the requisite medical examination; there is no standard exam process, and often reports reflect a preoccupation with determining virginity status; the doctor is not obligated to appear in court; court cases may be lengthy and are not necessarily *in camera* (private); and the application of laws, if not the laws themselves, often discriminates against survivors. Domestic violence cases are even more difficult to prosecute than rape cases. CCSL and CGG are working to improve the prosecutory process by variously providing case management to survivors and their families, sensitizing lawyers and members of the judiciary about GBV, and advocating for improved legislation.

Another significant local initiative aimed at addressing some of the reporting challenges facing GBV victims has been undertaken—almost single-handedly—by a senior female officer within the Sierra Leone police force. With support and guidance from an equally committed British officer of UNAMSIL, she has established a domestic violence police unit, created protocols and trainings for responding to victims of rape and domestic violence, and is instituting data collection of police reports relating to violence against women. The UNAMSIL representative is attempting to recruit trainers from Britain to lend technical assistance to the design of a hospital-based exam and counseling room for survivors. Both officers are soliciting funding to establish a safe house for victims, and both are working to create a collaborative relationship between health services, counseling programs, and police so that survivors can be more effectively and efficiently treated.

The United Nations Children's Fund (UNICEF) and the MSWGCA have assumed coordination for programming related to violence, and they have undertaken several media campaigns—with posters, radio jingles, etc.—to sensitize the community about sexual violence. Given the scope of their responsibilities, their oversight regarding GBV initiatives is limited and the predominant focus of their coordination is children and adolescents; programs targeting victims over eighteen have no special coordinating body. In fact, there appear to be few projects aimed at adult women survivors. Long-standing organizations such as the Italian NGO Cooperazione Internationale and Planned Parenthood Association of Sierra Leone (PPASL) have devised specific programs—assisted living, community activity centers, health awareness, and school fees—for child and adolescent survivors. The Irish NGO GOAL, whose project focusing on the welfare of street children and commercial sex workers provides outreach, sex education, transit shelters, and reintegration support to prostitutes, also reportedly works primarily with adolescents. None of these programs excludes women, but their emphases are nevertheless on younger populations.

This emphasis on children may in part reflect available funding streams. UNHCR recently retained a consultant to explore the possibility of developing a Sierra Leone Women's Initiative (SLWI), led by the Women's Forum and facilitated by UNHCR and the Brookings Initiative, to support and coordinate women's development projects. In her preliminary assessment, the consultant identified the lack of rehabilitation for survivors as an important gap to be rectified by the activities of the proposed SLWI. The consultant also identified the dearth of services outside of Freetown as a major limitation to addressing women's development in general and GBV specifically.[18]

Kenema

As in Freetown, the Kenema branch of FAWE was supported by MSF to work in collaboration with MSF, the International Committee of the Red Cross, the local branch of the MSWGCA, and Kenema hospital in the provision of medical triage and psychosocial services to approximately two thousand survivors of rape and domestic violence, mostly from the IDP camps in the Kenema area. Services were curtailed when MSF ceased to provide free medical services to victims in 2000, presumably in a strategy to support local fee-based treatment. FAWE representatives believe that the motivation for victims to come forward was stimulated by the availability of free medical care and that numbers will significantly decline without such an incentive. More recently, with assistance from the International Rescue

Committee (IRC), FAWE formalized GBV data collection and advocacy efforts, and has assumed the lead in consulting with elders, the police, lawyers, and the judiciary to develop GBV prevention and response protocols.

IRC's GBV program operates in three camps and two towns in the Kenema region. Its activities include case management, and health and counseling services for survivors; training for community-based counseling; data collection of GBV incidents; and basic GBV-related sensitization among local men and women leaders and community groups. They also facilitate leadership training and the development of women's camp councils; support construction of camp buildings for council meetings and survivor counseling; and provide coordination and resources for women's income-generating initiatives. The underlying goal of the IRC program has been to facilitate the development of local efforts to respond to the needs of survivors. Local women, including those living within the IDP camps, have been mobilized to provide supportive services. They have also been assisted in developing their advocacy skills, which enable them to raise awareness of and combat ongoing incidents of GBV. Many IDP women have not only experienced violence by the RUF or Westside Boys, they are additionally vulnerable to ongoing domestic violence as well as sexual abuse by men in their host community and within the camps. Notably, there were no reports of prostitution among the IDPs, though women's representatives in Freetown assert that prostitution is an inevitable outcome of impoverished camp conditions.

FAWE's and IRC's work is especially critical given the lack of GBV awareness among leaders in the Kenema area. Neither the local MSWGCA nor NCRRR representatives highlighted GBV as an area of concern. One representative even suggested that women coming forward to report rape were shaming themselves. Local police, as well, lack sensitivity to the issue and are generally not called upon to respond to incidents. There is currently no GBV coordination between local and international NGOs and local government officials. However, IRC and a local FAWE lawyer have taken steps to begin prosecution of rape cases. They have received initial support from local and national representatives, to the extent that a judge will be fielded from Freetown to preside locally over the cases. (Previously all cases had to be tried in Freetown.)

## Summary

As is the case in many conflict and post-conflict settings, war-related GBV in Sierra Leone has necessitated programmatic responses that have in turn raised awareness of GBV and strengthened local capacities to address the issue. Perhaps unique to Sierra Leone is the sheer number of local organizations interested in promoting women's development. During Sierra Leone's latest transition to peace, some of these organizations have been crucial in mobilizing communities and the government to recognize the rights and needs of survivors. In order to continue efforts to reduce violence against women, local NGOs will require increased technical and financial support. A consistent complaint from local NGO representatives is that international NGOs often create independent programs rather than partner with local organizations to provide services—such as the stand-alone trauma counseling program created by MSF and the street children program established by GOAL. The UNHCR-supported SLWI will presumably redress this problem by providing financing necessary to launch or continue local programming.

Even so, Sierra Leone women's organizations cannot operate effectively without a national infrastructure that supports the prevention of and response to GBV. The government's national plans for gender mainstreaming and the advancement of women represent an unprecedented effort in this direction, particularly to the extent that they call for the revision and expansion of laws relating to GBV. However, nationally supported collaboration related to GBV issues is an ongoing struggle. There have been no provisions instituted by the government to collect statistics from GBV service providers, though such statistics could clarify the maze of programming by identifying the populations currently receiving or requiring services as well as the nature of those services. Similarly, there is no national health policy mandating standard treatment protocols for survivors or exempting them from medical fees, in spite of clear indications from the FAWE/MSF collaborations that free services encourage survivors to seek medical treatment.

National programs, in turn, cannot be developed without international financial aid. In her recent visit to Sierra Leone, the U.N. Special Rapporteur on Violence Against Women concluded that the donor community is not responding appropriately to the needs of Sierra Leonean women. Freetown programs have generally focused on the needs of adolescent victims, specifically regarding war-related sexual abuse. Adult women have received less focused attention. Domestic violence, prostitution, and civilian rape are also lesser concerns, and though there are a few notable Sierra Leonean women advocating to reduce the practice of female genital excision, no programming currently exists. Populations outside of Freetown are reportedly not receiving GBV services, though there are organizations such as the Network Development for Justice and Rural Aid Sierra Leone which are interested in and prepared for fieldwork. Kenema and nearby Bo are exceptions given the presence of FAWE and IRC; their success may be a model for programming in other regions. In all programs, counseling services, though a popular intervention, tend to be the result of brief trainings and are themselves short term and informal. There are no provisions for counselor supervision or the ongoing development of treatment skills. Most projects, in fact, are based on short-term objectives. As Sierra Leone looks forward to transitioning from crisis to development strategies, GBV programming should evolve accordingly.

## Recommendations

1. International donors and NGOs must seek to provide support to national structures such as NCRRR and the government to address GBV on a broad scale. They should facilitate the MSWGCA's capacity to coordinate GBV prevention and response by participating in and, in some cases, leading coordination activities. Donors and NGOs must also provide local organizations with the financing and ability to address GBV at the community level, as well as to create a GBV advocacy base.

2. MSWGCA, responsible for implementing government polices on gender, must be supported to achieve the objectives outlined in the national plan. Local women's organizations should be solicited to participate in oversight and implementation. Service statistics on GBV should be submitted to relevant ministries and monitored and analyzed by MSWGCA. Nationwide media campaigns should educate the public regarding government policy and changing legislation.

3. The Ministry of the Interior must support the further sensitization of the police forces so that the activities already underway in Freetown can be implemented nationwide. Police must be held accountable for appropriate interventions and for the application of statutory laws. The judiciary must similarly be held accountable for upholding existing and evolving protections for survivors of GBV.

4. The Ministry of Health must remove obstacles to reporting violence by allowing no-fee rape exams, creating standard forensic reports, training forensic doctors in appropriate response, and supporting doctors' participation in court proceedings. All hospitals should be equipped with examination rooms and relevant medical equipment.

5. The NCRRR, if it is to fulfill its rehabilitation responsibilities, must include in its community-based projects objectives related to the prevention of and response to GBV. Similarly, the DDR policies, which currently do not acknowledge the needs of survivors of sexual assault, should introduce strategies for medical and psychosocial care.

6. International and local organizations—whether working in the community or in camps for the IDPs—should extend their programming to include GBV issues beyond war-related sexual assault, including domestic violence, prostitution, and harmful traditional practices. Local organizations should include men in their target population, whether as survivors of violence or as advocates for its reduction.

7. Respective ministries should sensitize local leaders about the necessity to address GBV, as well as about government policies. Local leaders should support the application of government polices in the prevention of GBV, so that the basic right to protection from GBV is not relative to local tradition.

## Notes

1  United Nations Office for the Coordination of Humanitarian Affairs (UNOCHA), *Consolidated Inter-Agency Appeal for Sierra Leone* (Freetown, 2001), 13.

2  UNOCHA, *Consolidated Inter-Agency Appeal for Sierra Leone*, 13.

3  L. Sumpter, "A Country that has 'Ceased to Exist,'" *The Fader* (n.d.): 153.

4  Physicians for Human Rights (PHR), *War-related Sexual Violence in Sierra Leone: A Population-based Assessment* (Boston, 2002), 3.

5  Amnesty International, *Rape and Other Form of Sexual Violence Against Girls and Women* (New York, 2000), 10.

6  U.S. Department of State, Bureau of Democracy, Human Rights, and Labor, *Female Genital Mutilation Background Paper* (Washington, D.C., 1997), 12.

7  Amnesty International, *Sierra Leone: Rape and Other Forms of Sexual Violence against Girls and Women* (Boston, 2000). See also: PHR, "Preliminary Findings and Recommendations," March 2000 Delegation to Sierra Leone, unpublished report.

8  Human Rights Watch, "Women in Conflict and Refugees," in *Human Rights Watch World Report 2000* (New York, 2000), 448.

9  Cited in Government of Sierra Leone, *Situation Analysis of Women and Children in Sierra Leone* (Freetown, 1999), 63.

10  A. Coker and D. Richter, "Violence Against Women in Sierra Leone: Frequency and Correlates of Intimate Partner Violence and Forced Sexual Intercourse" *African Journal of Reproductive Health*, 2, No. 1 (1998): 65.

11  PHR, *War-related Sexual Violence in Sierra Leone*, 9.

12  Government of Sierra Leone, *Situation Analysis of Women and Children in Sierra Leone*, 121.

13  Ministry of Social Welfare, Gender, and Children's Affairs (MSWGCA), *National Policy on Gender Mainstreaming* (Freetown, 2001), 3.

14  World Health Organization, *HIV/AIDS in Sierra Leone: The Future Is at Stake, The Strategic and Organisational Context and Recommendations for Action* (Freetown, 2000), 2.

15  MSWGCA, *National Policy on the Advancement of Women* (Freetown, 2001), 4.

16  U.S. Department of State, *Sierra Leone Country Report on Human Rights Practices* (Washington, D.C., 2000), 8.

17  U.S. Department of State, *Sierra Leone Country Report on Human Rights Practices*, 7.

18  United Nations High Commissioner for Refugees, *Mission Report on Sexual and Gender-based Violence Programming Support to Sierra Leone: Reintegration with Equality* (Geneva, 2000), 19.

Country Profiles from Asia

*Afghanistan / Pakistan*
*Burma / Thailand*
*East Timor*

# Situation in *Afghanistan* and Among Afghan Refugees in *Pakistan*

April 14-21, 2001

*Author's note: This report represents circumstances as they existed during an April 2001 research visit to Pakistan. Although the situation of Afghans, including refugees, has changed dramatically since the events of September 11, 2001, this report's findings and recommendations regarding GBV remain relevant. With the fall of the Taliban regime, the Pakistan and Afghan governments, as well as the humanitarian aid and civil sectors, are able to declaim publicly and aggressively the widespread nature of GBV among the Afghan population and institute appropriate programming to address its prevention and response.*

## Background

### Historical Context

In significant measure, the past twenty-two years of Afghanistan's history have been a history of exploitation: by cold war superpowers waging a proxy war; by neighboring governments exploiting Afghanistan's geographic position to pursue regional interests; and by internal factions competing for hegemony over Afghanistan's multi-ethnic population. The first wave of conflict began in the late 1970s with increasing internal opposition to Afghanistan's ruling elite; against this backdrop of political instability the Soviet Union invaded in 1979. The ensuing ten years of war—during which Afghanistan's economy of rural subsistence was all but destroyed and replaced by black market monetization and dependence on international humanitarian aid—resulted in thousands of casualties and precipitated the flight of millions to refugee camps in Pakistan and Iran. The conflict also resulted in an agglomeration of rebel Islamist groups (collectively referred to as the Mujahideen) that during the cold war was financed primarily by the U.S. and Europe and supported logistically by Iran and Pakistan. Three years after the formal 1989 Soviet withdrawal from the war, which Russian

president Mikhail Gorbachev characterized as a "bleeding wound," members of the Mujahideen succeeded in overtaking Afghanistan's capital city of Kabul and instituting a nominal Islamic government.[1]

Factional disputes, which caused pervasive violence among the Mujahideen and against the civilian population, severely undermined the new government's stability, credibility, and popularity, so that when a group of mostly rural Pashtun Islamic fundamentalists, referring to themselves as the Taliban, emerged as a military force, they were able to fight and buy their way to power relatively quickly. With primary support from a Pakistan invested in preserving Afghanistan as a strategic neighbor in its tense stand-off with India, the Taliban moved from the south to capture Kabul in 1996, and under leader Mullah Mohammad Omar proclaimed control of the newly declared Islamic Emirate of Afghanistan. Meanwhile, members of the ousted Mujahideen, including President Burhanuddin Rabbani and his military commander Ahmed Shah Massood, regrouped to form an opposition Northern Alliance, also referred to as the United Front. Primarily comprised of Tajik, Uzbek, and ethnic Hazara minorities, and backed by Iran, Russia, Tajikistan, and Uzbekistan, the United Front progressively lost control of all but 10 percent of

Afghanistan, retaining pockets in Afghanistan's central highlands, in the northeast, and in the frontline of combat north of Kabul.

In place of a constitution, Taliban leaders issued edicts curtailing even the most basic human rights. Their Islamic courts and religious police, the Ministry for the Promotion of Virtue and Suppression of Vice (PVSV), were established to enforce violently and summarily the Taliban's ultra-conservative interpretations of Islamic law. These practices, the trafficking of drugs and terrorism, and other isolationist and reactionary policies of Taliban leaders engendered the enmity of world powers. When the Taliban refused to facilitate the handover of Osama bin Laden, the suspected mastermind behind the 1998 attacks on U.S. embassies in Kenya and Tanzania, the U.S. responded with cruise missile strikes on alleged terrorist training camps near the Pakistan border, and the United Nations drafted a resolution imposing international sanctions on Afghanistan. Although targeted at the Taliban, the 1999 sanctions further isolated the whole of Afghanistan. Ongoing internal skirmishes between the Taliban and United Front, whose indiscriminate military tactics led to high rates of civilian death, plus the effects of severe drought, resulted in the internal displacement of a half to one million Afghans, and a refugee population that, as of April 2001, was estimated at around three million, 75 percent of whom were women and children.[2]

Those who fled Afghanistan left a country with some of the most dire health conditions in the world. Infant and maternal mortality are at global highs; life expectancy is 43 years for men and 44 for women[3]; clean water is unavailable to the majority of the population; and vast networks of landmines and unexploded ordnance not only pose immediate threats to life and limb but also limit agricultural production and contribute to high rates of malnutrition.[4] Those who fled Afghanistan also left behind a country with some of the worst human rights abuses in the world. In Taliban-controlled areas, PVSV reportedly carried out stonings, floggings, public executions, extrajudicial murder, and amputations of those in violation of Taliban edicts. For women and girls, the Taliban decrees have been especially devastating.

## Status of Women in Afghanistan

In the years before and during the Soviet occupation, Afghan women enjoyed increased access to the public sphere, including education, professional training, and work, but their liberties were rescinded with the rise of the Mujahideen. Violence against women, especially in Kabul, was pervasive during the Mujahideen's unstable rule, such that the Taliban's police state initially provided a welcome reprieve.[5] However, the Taliban's subsequent and consistent denial of women's rights resulted in some of the most extreme discriminatory regulations against women in the world: girls were officially prohibited from attending school beyond the primary level (female literacy rates are estimated as low as 4 percent[6]); women required accompaniment by a male family member and a cloth sheath (*burqa* or *chadari*) covering their entire body when in public; houses with female occupants had to have opaque windows; and women were forbidden to work outside the home in anything but agriculture and health services, and specifically forbidden from most positions with international agencies, where salaried work is concentrated. The enforced sex segregation of health workers resulted in a drastic reduction in the quality and availability of treatment for women, effectively preventing many women from receiving health care. Although the implementation of these regulations varied widely—tending to be more extreme in Taliban-controlled urban areas—profound institutional and practical discrimination against women nevertheless existed throughout Afghanistan, even in areas controlled by the United Front.[7]

## Status of Afghan Women in Pakistan

Unfortunately, for many women who seek refuge in the camps along Pakistan's border with Afghanistan, conditions—by international standards—are only marginally better than inside Afghanistan. The government of Pakistan originally afforded Afghan refugees fleeing the Soviet occupation *prima facie* refugee status, but in 1995 Pakistan officially discontinued its refugee assistance programs. In 1999 Pakistan rescinded refugee status to newly arriving or re-entering Afghans, whose impetus for migration was perceived as economic rather than political. As of 2001, Afghans without appropriate visas were subject to deportation under the Foreigners Act, though as yet Pakistan has not widely enforced this rule. The government's Commissionerate for Afghan Refugees (CAR) cooperates with the United Nations High Commissioner for Refugees (UNHCR) and other partners in the provision of protection, education, and health care, but international aid is grossly insufficient to meet basic needs. Although limited assistance is still available to registered refugees in established camps, conditions can be extremely harsh for newer arrivals, and the general climate in Pakistan is unfavorable to refugees, particularly those who are not of ethnic Pashtun origin.

In addition to the lack of assistance and legal rights, refugee women are also affected by continued gender discrimination. The strong presence of the Taliban along Pakistan's border and especially in the Pashtun-dominated Northwest Frontier Province (NWFP)—where 127 of Pakistan's 203 refugee camps are located—continues to buttress the Taliban's declaration that Afghans are nowhere exempt from their edicts. As such, many Afghan refugee women living in Pakistan's refugee camps—and the local and international organizations that assist them—experience severe constraints to their activity and mobility. The marginal status of refugees, compounded by the pervasive discriminatory attitudes against women in Pakistan, significantly inhibits women's access to basic assistance or protection. Refugee women's limited recourse has an acute impact on their vulnerability to GBV.

## Gender-based Violence

### Afghanistan

The Taliban edicts that controlled virtually all spheres of women's lives were a widespread form of institutionalized GBV, reinforced by threats, arbitrary beatings in the street, and formal public lashings by the religious police.[8] Although Afghanistan is a signatory to the Convention on the Elimination of All Forms of Discrimination Against Women (CEDAW), the Taliban rendered that commitment meaningless. In their 2001 investigation of the perceptions and impact of Taliban edicts on Afghan women, Physicians for Human Rights (PHR) found that an overwhelming majority of women—and men—did not support Taliban restrictions on women's human rights. In Taliban controlled areas, women interviewed by PHR reported high rates of depression and correspondingly high rates of suicidal ideation and suicide attempts, which interviewees largely attributed to the effects of Taliban oppression.[9]

Even before the Taliban, particularly in rural areas where tribal customs predominated, patriarchal tradi-

tions flourished; those traditions form the basis of the gender discrimination that defines current policies and practices. As repositories of family honor, women and girls have historically been held responsible for abuses committed against them. Under Taliban regulations, unless women reporting rape could prove non-compliance by producing four male witnesses, they were at risk of harsh punishment for fornication and adultery. In fact, repercussions were egregious regardless of whether the sexual conduct was mutually consenting. Not surprisingly, women had no systems for reporting violence or receiving assistance. Apparently the most viable option for an unmarried girl exposed as having had sexual relations was to marry her partner, even if the man had perpetrated the rape. In more severe resolutions, a girl—or woman—and her perpetrator would be killed by the offended family.

In the resulting culture of silence, it is very difficult to determine the extent of war-related or other sexual violence committed against Afghan women. Even so, rape and abductions have been widely acknowledged as an endemic feature of the post-Soviet rise of the Mujahideen.[10] In the years following the Taliban takeover, rates of sexual violence were perceived to have generally decreased. However, human rights organizations have provided anecdotal evidence of ongoing violence, including rape, abductions, and forced marriages carried out by both the Taliban and the United Front, particularly on the front lines. Human Rights Watch recorded accounts of Taliban fighters systematically sexually assaulting and abducting ethnic minority women in the northwest city of Mazar-I-Sharif during its takeover in 1998. In her 1999 visit to Pakistan and Afghanistan, the U.N. Special Rapporteur on Violence Against Women received reports of Taliban abuse—including abduction and forced marriages—of ethnic Hazara and Tajik women perceived to be sympathetic to opposition forces.[11]

There are indications—based on research and commentary by investigators and NGOs operating in Pakistan—that other forms of GBV such as child abuse, trafficking for prostitution, and domestic violence have been perpetrated in Afghanistan. In a 1998 reproductive health survey by the International Rescue Committee (IRC) of over two hundred women living in camps south of Peshawar, Pakistan, 79 percent acknowledged being beaten by husbands, 39 percent by other family members, and 13.4

percent reported that men have the right to beat their wives. Notably, some of the women surveyed also mentioned that violence against them had decreased since becoming refugees. Additional qualitative research by IRC on child sexual abuse carried out in 2001 revealed a case in which a sixteen-year-old Kabul girl, whose father was imprisoned for life after the girl twice reported incest to the authorities, was also imprisoned for four years on the grounds that she should have stopped the abuse earlier.[12] In another incident reported by the Special Rapporteur, a twelve-year-old Afghan girl separated from her parents was trafficked to Pakistan and sold to a Punjabi man.[13]

### Pakistan

The Special Rapporteur also reported concerns about the apparent rise in GBV among the refugee population in Pakistan, where the lack of assistance and protections offered by the government of Pakistan have exacerbated harmful traditional practices and introduced new forms of violence. Despite IRC's 1998 findings that domestic violence decreased for women living in camps, the Special Rapporteur found in 1999 that fatalities in domestic disputes were on the rise, likely resulting from family tensions associated with the precarious status of refugees and high rates of unemployment.[14] Situational and economically driven early marriages may also be increasing; in one camp outside Peshawar, women freely admitted that selling their prepubescent daughters to Pakistani men provided a source of income and was preferable to the child's return to Afghanistan. In some cases, Pakistani security forces within the camp facilitate this process.

Evidence further indicates that Afghan refugee women and girls—and boys—are vulnerable to child sexual abuse, prostitution, and trafficking. In IRC's 2001 research, one camp resident claimed "it was not uncommon for men to rape girls, even in the presence of their wives."[15] Other reports suggest that prostitution of women and girls is facilitated inside the camps by family members, camp leadership, and camp security. Camp security has also been implicated by female refugees in the rape and abduction of encamped women and girls, though these crimes are not reported because of survivors' fears of being harassed or deported by Pakistani police.

Refugee women living outside the camps may be at even greater risk of sexual exploitation, especially if they are widowed or otherwise without male protection; scenarios include forced prostitution by their neighbors or employers, or elective prostitution as a method for supporting their children in an environment that otherwise offers no economic resources. Boys are also at risk, in part because of their comparative visibility and mobility, and in part because of traditions that may lead to their sexual exploitation. In Afghan wedding ceremonies, for example, entertainment may include dancing boys ceremoniously dressed as girls, who in some cases sexually service male guests.[16] Prostitution by young boys exists throughout Pakistan, and it is likely that in the border areas Afghan children are represented.

## Current GBV-related Programming

### The Refugee Population in Pakistan

Although the extent of GBV against Afghan women and children is alarming, the lack of GBV-related services for the refugee community may be even more so. In part, this lack is owing to the constraints imposed by the Taliban along the border. It is also the result of the prevailing disregard for violence against women in Pakistani culture and practice. According to a 1999 Human Rights Watch investigation, "Women in Pakistan face staggeringly high rates of rape, sexual assault, and domestic violence while their attackers largely go unpunished owing to rampant incompetence, corruption, and biases against women throughout the criminal justice system."[17] As in Afghanistan, Pakistan's Hudood Ordinances place women at risk of prosecution if they fail to prove rape allegations, such that men may be acquitted for rape while their victims are held on grounds of fornication and adultery: an estimated one-third of women jailed in Peshawar in 1998 were awaiting trial for adultery.[18] Doctors are ill-trained to conduct forensic exams, often focusing their examination on the virginity status of the victim. Statutory rape is not a crime, nor is rape in marriage. Domestic violence is also not explicitly criminalized in the Pakistani legal code and "virtually never" investigated by police.[19] Special women's police stations that were established in 1994 to avert the problem of police abuses against women—including rape—are too poorly funded to operate effectively.[20] Trafficking in women "is protected by powerful criminal interests and operates relatively openly," with little effort by the government to stem the tide of the estimated thousands of women who arrive annually from Bangladesh, Afghanistan, Burma, Sri Lanka, and India.[21]

In this climate of impunity, it is virtually impossible for Afghan women refugees to seek redress for gender-based crimes committed against them, even by Pakistani perpetrators. Nor are they generally able to gain access to palliative services. No health care providers working within camps have clear protocols for addressing violence, and no psychosocial programs exist for camp-based refugees that target the issue of GBV. Outside of the camps the situation is only marginally improved. Although GBV-related services are not widely available to refugees, several local Pakistani NGOs provide medical and psychosocial support to victims of violence from which refugees may benefit. In the NWFP, select Afghan women's NGOs working explicitly on issues affecting Afghan refugee women have developed informal networks to address victims of violence. However, their need to operate under the radar of the Taliban and their ability to provide anything other than general emotional support has restricted their impact. Any protective services available to refugees are the result of UNHCR's initiative, and yet the fact that field-based protection officers are, by necessity, men, curtails the extent to which women may seek assistance. In spite of these limitations, select programming that touches—even if only peripherally—on issues of violence against Afghan women is moving forward.

## Islamabad

Pakistan's capital city of Islamabad is home to the head offices of most of the international institutions serving refugees. UNHCR's "Women at Risk" project facilitates resettlement for the most vulnerable Afghan women, many of whom are widows and are in danger of or have experienced sexual exploitation. The project collaborates with IRC, which in turn partners with local NGOs. UNHCR also collaborates with two safe houses in Islamabad to ensure women's security during the transition to resettlement. In one case referred for resettlement, an Afghan woman's widowhood led her to work as a domestic servant, which in turn led to repeated rapes committed by her employer against both the woman and her daughter.

The United Nations Population Fund (UNFPA) has

also cooperated with UNHCR in the provision of refugee health care, of which prevention and response to GBV is a stated objective. To meet that objective, UNFPA has supported inconspicuous, brief presentations to Afghan men on the prevention and consequences of GBV. The International Organization for Migration (IOM) is currently working with the Pakistani authorities to develop a strategy for information campaigns addressing trafficking.

A few exemplary local organizations in Islamabad have worked with Afghan survivors of GBV to address their health and psychosocial needs—though in all cases the refugees are not their primary target population. For example, the Pakistani NGO Struggle for Change (SACH) provides rehabilitation and training for survivors of torture through psychotherapy, physiotherapy, and socioeconomic support. It also has an education program for survivors' children, most of whom are Afghan. The women's rights organization Savera provides similarly broad-based services, which are accessible to refugee women victims of violence. Rozan, a comprehensive NGO that provides training and direct services addressing multiple aspects of women's psychosocial health, gender, and GBV also occasionally receives counseling referrals for Afghan refugee women. The children's rights organization Sahil has facilitated education to refugees on child sexual abuse and has been critical in monitoring and publicizing abuse against children in Pakistan.

## Peshawar

The largest city in the NWFP, Peshawar serves as a base of operation for many international and local NGOs working with refugee populations in camps and urban areas along the Pakistan-Afghanistan border. The UNHCR "Women at Risk" program has activities in Peshawar, as does its IRC partner program. Peshawar's UNHCR community services officer was a strong advocate for developing programming to combat GBV in the camps, and served as advisor to an exemplary but short-term effort by IRC to address GBV. Initially conceived to target violence against women, the IRC project generated security concerns and the focus was therefore shifted to research and training on sexual violence against Afghan children, of which education on general issues of GBV was one component. The Women's Commission for Refugee Women and Children (Women's Commission) supports a Peshawar-based technical advisor to work on broad-based gender issues among Afghans in Afghanistan and Pakistan. The advisor's training, monitoring, and advocacy activities have improved programming for and sensitivity to Afghan women in multiple ways. By highlighting and addressing women's vulnerabilities, the advisor's activities have also acted as a preventive measure against GBV.

Many of the support services available to women refugees exist through local Afghan women's NGOs. None of the programs has specific activities targeting GBV, but several have components that directly or indirectly benefit survivors. The Afghan Women's Council (AWC), which runs health, education, and advocacy programs for refugees, also takes testimony from widows of war and publishes it in a newsletter distributed to women in Afghanistan. This sharing of information provides an opportunity for women— many of whom have experienced some form of GBV—to receive support, and it decreases the silence around the issue of GBV. Because the AWC has heard so many accounts of domestic violence, it is hoping to create support groups and discussion forums for abused spouses. The Center for Street Children and Women (CSCW) has a model component project, Madadgar, that provides supportive services and referrals for "women in crisis," some of whom have been victims of domestic violence, forced prostitution, and sexual harassment. Because CSCW has multiple services such as skills training, medical care, education, and recreation, it can refer women both internally as well as to other organizations with which it networks.

Remarkably, in a political climate hostile to women's rights, a number of organizations at both the international and local level have very active and sophisticated gender training and education programs. International organizations such as Norwegian Church Aid (NCA) and the Swedish Committee for Afghanistan (SCA) subtly incorporate issues of violence against women in their gender trainings, which they provide to large numbers of employees working in both Pakistan and Afghanistan. Local organizations similarly committed to gender training and education include the Center for Humanitarian Affairs and the Cooperation Center for Afghanistan. Although neither has curricula that directly address violence against women, each organization has expressed a desire to expand training to incorporate GBV more overtly. This desire to attend to GBV more overtly is common among agencies serving Afghan women, sounding a clarion call to those invested in promoting the health and welfare of the Afghan refugee community.

## Summary

GBV in Afghanistan may qualify as among the most pervasive—and certainly among the most institutionalized—in the world. Evidence from researchers and human rights advocates suggests that GBV in refugee communities living in Pakistan is similarly pervasive, where the predominant cultures of violence toward women and hostility toward refugees may further exacerbate its prevalence. Despite this evidence, few humanitarian organizations have taken up the issue—largely because of legitimate security concerns within Afghanistan and along Pakistan's western border. Even so, there are several initiatives at both the international and local levels that have successfully, if discreetly and indirectly, addressed GBV. The more vocal and visible are those operating in Islamabad that primarily serve the Pakistani community, such as SACH, Savera, Sahil, and Rozan. However, IRC's research on child sexual abuse, AWC's testimony collection, CSCW's crisis response project, and the gender trainings of NCA and SCA each illustrate the viability of developing GBV programming that specifically targets Afghans, even in the more conservative NWFP.

The above projects may act as models to the many organizations that have not yet instituted GBV activities but have expressed the need, as well as the desire, to confront more aggressively violence against refugee women. Among them is the Committee for the Defense of Afghan Women's Rights (Rawzana), which would like to implement trainings on legal rights for survivors. The Afghan Women's Resource Center would like to incorporate GBV prevention and response into their existing literacy, skills training, and health services for urban and camp-based women. Marie Stopes Society, a local affiliate of Marie Stopes International, would like their doctors working inside camps in the NWFP and their health workers serving urban refugees to receive training in responding to GBV. The local Peshawar organization AWARD participates in a Pakistani violence against women forum, of which the Peshawar police commissioner is supportive. AWARD does not currently engage with the refugee community, but it is hoping to develop a training manual on GBV and would like to collaborate with Afghan NGOs for its implementation. Other Pakistani NGOs, such as those operating in Islamabad, also have expertise and materials available on issues of violence against women that could be made accessible to international and local organizations wishing to target refugee populations.

Interestingly, a common concern articulated by local organizations was not centered on issues of security but rather on the availability of international organizations to assist, both in terms of technical support and funding, in the development of GBV initiatives. Perhaps because local organizations are accustomed to working in covert ways to promote and deliver services, they feel relatively confident in their ability to design and institute measures to address GBV. The immediate barrier, it would seem, is one of donor support and international commitment.

## Recommendations

1. The donor community should examine its commitment to addressing the health and safety needs of the refugee population and, acknowledging the major impact of GBV on morbidity and mortality, it should finance the institutionalization of broad-based health and other support services to assist survivors, as well as initiatives to reduce the prevalence of violence. These services should be instituted not only in Pakistan but also in Afghanistan to meet the needs of returning refugees and the population at large.

2. UNHCR, in collaboration with members of the CAR in Pakistan and with the newly appointed Minister for Women's Affairs (Dr. Sima Samar) in Afghanistan, should support the development of Afghanistan- and Pakistan-based coordinating bodies to examine and address GBV for both the refugee and returnee populations. The coordinating bodies should operate within their respective countries as a forum for multi-sectoral collaboration, and each body should include members of the Pakistan and Afghan governments, UN representatives, religious and community leaders, and international and local NGOs working with refugee women. The coordinating bodies should also provide security for participating local NGOs which may be at risk by more conserva-

tive members of the Islamic community. The forums should have a long-term plan for moving to national government oversight.

3. UNHCR and international NGOs should develop mechanisms for assessing and recording the nature and prevalence of GBV among populations served. They should use that data to bring pressure to bear on the Pakistan government to implement greater protections for women refugees according to the mandate of international refugee protection and according to the Pakistan government's commitment to addressing GBV as a signatory to CEDAW. Any and all efforts of data collection must have mechanisms to ensure absolute confidentiality so as to protect both the survivor and those collecting data.

4. The Pakistan government should take a strong stance against the exploitation and rape of refugee women by Pakistani police and authorities. Similarly, mechanisms should be instituted immediately by the government of Afghanistan to ensure broad-based legal protections for returning women that include safe corridors for return, as well as the availability of protections after repatriation.

5. Religious and community leaders in Afghanistan and along the border of Pakistan should be engaged in the design of widespread education campaigns that incorporate Islamic teachings to promote the prevention of GBV and illustrate the extent to which violence against women is anathema to Islam. Of particular importance to any education efforts will be addressing community attitudes that overwhelmingly "blame the victim."

6. Ministries responsible for social welfare, internal affairs, and the judiciary in both Pakistan and Afghanistan should require trainings within their respective sectors on the existence and application of protective laws. Women should be actively recruited to the police forces, and in Pakistan existing women's police precincts should receive more operational support. Female police officers should be placed in Pakistan's refugee camps. Ministries should require that sex-disaggregated data on violence is collected and monitored at local and national levels.

7. Pakistan's CAR, in collaboration with UNFPA, should significantly expand its health response protocols for refugees to include GBV activities. Standard trainings on all aspects of GBV, including forensic examinations, screening of clients for histories of abuse, and ensuring doctor-patient confidentiality, should be required by CAR for health staff. Efforts should be made to increase the numbers of Afghan health workers in the camps, and to ensure that the current Pakistani health providers are able to speak Dari and Pashto, and can communicate effectively with members of minority groups, including Uzbeks and Turkmen, who may not speak Dari or Pashto. International NGOs with health programs in Afghanistan should similarly introduce protocols to screen for and examine survivors.

8. International NGOs operating in Pakistan and Afghanistan should create and implement strategies for incorporating GBV prevention and response into existing education, skills-building, and psychosocial projects. International NGOs should support local partner organizations to do the same. In Pakistan, expert Pakistani NGOs working in the area of GBV should be called upon to facilitate this goal. Shelters that have been extremely successful in Islamabad should be replicated in the NWFP and in Afghanistan.

9. Local and international NGOs should research and introduce projects that address the concerns of boys, particularly their sexual exploitation. Projects developed in Afghanistan for men—such as demobilization and reintegration activities—should include GBV prevention and response in their education and direct services, as well as psychological and drug-abuse counseling.

## Notes

1 M. Fielden, and J. Goodhand, "Beyond the Taliban: The Afghan Conflict and United Nations Peacekeeping," *Conflict, Security, and Development*, 1:3 (2001), 5-32.

2 U.S. Department of State, *Country Reports on Human Rights Practices: Afghanistan* (Washington D.C., 2001), 2.

3 Physicians for Human Rights (PHR), *Women's Health and Human Rights in Afghanistan: A Population-based Assessment* (Boston, 2001), 3.

4 U.S. Department of State, *Country Reports on Human Rights Practices: Afghanistan*, 12.

5 Oxfam U.K., "Gender and Afghanistan" (unpublished document, Oxford, 2001), 3.

6 U.S. Department of State, *Country Reports on Human Rights Practices: Afghanistan*, 13.

7 United Nations, *Report of the Special Rapporteur on Violence Against Women, Mission to Pakistan and Afghanistan* (Geneva, 2000), 5.

8 Human Rights Watch, *Humanity Denied: Systematic Violations of Women's Rights in Afghanistan* (New York, 2001), 8.

9 PHR, *Women's Health and Human Rights in Afghanistan*, 8-13.

10 A. Pont, *Blind Chickens and Social Animals: Creating Space for Afghan Women's Narratives Under the Taliban*, Report for Mercy Corps, (Portland, 2001), 48.

11 U.N., *Report of the Special Rapporteur*, 5.

12 C. McGinn, "Sexual Abuse of Afghan Refugee Children in Northwest Pakistan: Patterns, Perceptions, and Response" (unpublished report for the International Rescue Committee, Peshawar, 2001), 10.

13 U.N., *Report of the Special Rapporteur*, 11.

14 U.N., *Report of the Special Rapporteur*, 11.

15 McGinn, *Sexual Abuse of Afghan Refugee Children in Northwest Pakistan*, 8.

16 McGinn, *Sexual Abuse of Afghan Refugee Children in Northwest Pakistan*, 13.

17 Human Rights Watch, *Crime or Custom?: Violence Against Women in Pakistan* (New York, 1999), 1.

18 U.S. Department of State, *Country Reports on Human Rights Practices: Afghanistan*, 5.

19 Human Rights Watch, *Crime or Custom?*, 40.

20 U.S. Department of State, *Country Reports on Human Rights Practices: Afghanistan*, 4.

21 U.S. Department of State, *Country Reports on Human Rights Practices: Afghanistan*, 21.

# Situation in
# *Burma*
# and Among Burmese Refugees in
# *Thailand*

April 22-29, 2001

## Background

### Historical Context

Rather than being notable for its diverse ethnic history and rich natural resources, Burma is distinct as the setting of one of the longest-running civil wars in the world. Declared independent from British rule in 1948, Burma's pro-democracy leaders were assassinated even before their Union of Burma was officially established. In a post-independence leadership vacuum, internal conflicts escalated along political and ethnic lines: between democratic and communist militants, as well as between majority Burmans (who comprise approximately 65 percent of total Burmese) and several of the larger of Burma's over one hundred minority groups, including the Mon, Shan, Chin, Karen, and Rohingya (each distinguished by language, cultural and religious traditions, and adaptation to their physical environment). In March 1963 a military coup replaced the unstable civilian government with one-party rule. The policies instituted by Burman dictator General Ne Win included the "Burmese Way to Socialism," which prescribed a nationalized economy and the diversion of natural and human resources to support an expanding military machine, and a "Four Cuts Campaign," in which food, information, money, and rebel recruits were aggressively withdrawn or diverted from villages opposed to the junta.

As minority communities were increasingly dislocated and villages disrupted by economic and political tyranny, many formerly divided insurgency groups united in the National League for Democracy (NLD).

The NLD's historic 1988 demonstrations were met with indiscriminate state violence in which thousands of anti-government protesters were killed. In 1990 the military junta bowed to public pressure for democratic elections, but when 80 percent of the popular vote went to the NLD and its leader, Nobel Peace Prize Laureate Aung San Suu Kyi, the government responded by placing Suu Kyi under house arrest and further escalating military aggression.

Belying its self-appointed title as the State Peace and Development Council (SPDC), Burma's current military regime has neither brokered peace nor stimulated development. Although cease-fires have been negotiated with some fifteen insurgent groups since 1989, widespread state-sponsored human rights abuses remain the violent norm.[1] Burma ranks among the poorest countries in the world; its schools and health system have collapsed; and it is home to a rapidly escalating AIDS epidemic—thanks in part to the fact that Burma has become one of the largest producers of heroin in the world. Ongoing internal skirmishes, military repression of ethnic minorities, forced relocations based on economic strategy, and pervasive poverty have resulted in a constant exodus of political and economic refugees.

### Refugee Situation in Thailand

It is impossible even to approximate the number of internally displaced inside Burma. However, recent estimates of the total number of Burmese who in the last fifteen years have fled to neighboring countries hover around 1.5 million.[2] About 9 percent live in refugee camps along the Thai/Burma border, primarily representing the Karen, Karenni, and Mon ethnic groups.[3] A loose estimate of another several hundred thousand Burmese—inclusive of the ethnic Shan, who have been categorically denied refugee services by the Royal Thai Government (RTG) because of their perceived status as economic refugees—are reported to be living throughout Thailand as "illegal immigrants." Reflecting the global refugee phenomenon, women and girls account for 60 to 80 percent of the Burmese refugee population.

The RTG, whose country's resources and land have been drained by the seemingly intractable refugee crisis, has imposed increasingly severe restrictions on the rights and mobility of Burmese living in Thailand. The protections available to refugees are at best ambiguous and, often, imperiled. Because the RTG has not signed the 1951 United Nations Convention Relating to the Status of Refugees, no Burmese living in Thailand are officially recognized under international refugee law. Only "persons of concern," those evaluated by the RTG as direct victims of Burmese conflict, are officially permitted to receive humanitarian aid, primarily within camp settings. Thus, ethnic Burmese entering Thailand from regions in Burma that are not officially designated as conflict areas are denied services and live under the threat of forced repatriation, despite the fact that their political, civil, and economic rights have been repeatedly disavowed by the SPDC and Burmese military even after declarations of cease-fires.

Food and relief assistance to refugees living in camps is coordinated by the Burmese Border Consortium (BBC), "in cooperation with the RTG and in accordance with the regulations of the Thai Ministry of Interior (MOI)."[4] BBC also cooperates with humanitarian aid partners which provide health and education services. The MOI oversees policing of the camps and refugee compliance in general. Within the last three years, the RTG has enlisted the support of the United Nations High Commissioner for Refugees (UNHCR), whose mandate is registering, monitoring, and protecting refugees within camps and those who are newly arriving or who are being relocated from one refugee camp to another. UNHCR is also responsible for identifying and assisting "persons of concern" in urban areas. However, since the RTG's 1999 crackdown on "illegal immigrants," those judged by UNHCR (but not by the

Thai government) to be "persons of concern" may be at increased risk of forced return to Burma.

The limited mandate of UNHCR, the active surveillance of MOI representatives within and without the camps, the necessity of the BBC and its partners to act in accordance with RTG policy, and the failure of the RTG to recognize the rights of all Burmese refugees—together have important implications for survivors of GBV.

## Gender-based Violence

### Burma

According to the international NGO Images Asia's review of the Burmese government's compliance with the United Nations Convention on the Elimination of All Forms of Discrimination Against Women (CEDAW) (ratified by Burma in 1997):

> Women have been victims of the well-documented and pervasive human rights abuses also suffered by men, including forced labor on government construction projects, forced portering for the army, summary arrest, torture and extra-judicial execution. These and other human rights violations are committed sometimes in the course of military operations, but more often as part of the army's policy of repression of ethnic minority civilians. Women and girls are specifically targeted for rape and sexual harassment by soldiers. *Many of the areas in Burma where soldiers rape women are not areas of active conflict, though they may have large numbers of standing troops.* There has been little action on the part of the state to reduce the prevalence of sexual abuse by its military personnel or ensure that the perpetrators of these crimes are brought to justice.[5] (Emphasis added.)

As this and other human rights reports attest, Burma is no exception to the rule of military violence against women and girls during conflict. Burma is exceptional, however, in that its military includes the highest number of child soldiers in the world. Use of child soldiers is itself an abuse, and may also be a factor in the abuses committed by the state against the civilian population: children can be more easily manipulated or forced to commit atrocities.

Testimony by survivors and witnesses of military aggression includes reports of gang rape, forced genital penetration by knives and other objects, mutilation of breasts and genitals, and more. Another striking aspect of the state violence perpetrated against women in Burma is that it is not limited to conflict zones; rather, it is an unsparing and unrestrained component of the Burmese military's state-supported reign over ethnic minority civilians. In her comprehensive account of sexual violence perpetrated by the Burmese military, Betsy Apple attributes the culture and prevalence of rape, enslavement, coerced sex, forced prostitution, and forced marriage to a "hierarchy of domination," in which violence, oppression, and exploitation are institutionalized military values, ultimately finding their target among the most vulnerable and disempowered: the bodies of ethnic minority women and girls.[6]

The notion of Burmese women's disempowerment runs counter to the SPDC official stance that in Burma "there is no gender disparity in personal relationships" and "women are accorded equal rights with men."[7] Images Asia's CEDAW review quoted above argues otherwise, suggesting that in virtually all spheres, women are subordinate to men and subject to related gender-based abuses of power. Women victims of sexual harassment and violence within their communities or domestic violence in the home have limited legal recourse or community resources: police and the judiciary are both unreliable and not trusted, and social tradition and family pressure conspire to discourage reporting or otherwise acknowledging abuse.[8]

Prostitution inside Burma has reportedly increased dramatically as a result of the civil war, as has sex trafficking of migrants.[9] In addition to the prevailing culture of men frequenting prostitutes, widespread sexual violence within Burma, the associated stigma of losing one's virginity before marriage, and the breakdown of traditional family structures have precipitated the rise in women and girls entering the sex industry; another precipitant is certainly the lack of economic options, particularly for ethnic Burmese women living in rural areas. In 1997 the World Health Organization estimated the female illiteracy rate within Burma to be 70 percent. Despite the Burmese government's stated commitment to improving female access to education, subsequent calculations place the illiteracy rate even higher, at 80 percent, among women living in conflict zones or remote areas.[10] It is not surprising that of the estimated forty thousand Burmese women trafficked each year into Thailand's factories, brothels, and domestic work, those at greatest risk are reportedly women from remote regions of Burma.[11]

## Thailand

GBV against Burmese refugees in Thailand is as difficult to quantify as violence against women inside Burma. Thailand-based Burmese women's organizations periodically release information on the sexual subjugation and exploitation of women by the Thai military, police, and immigration officials, at checkpoints and border crossings, detention centers, brothels, and in and surrounding camps.[12] One contributing factor to the perpetuation of such violence is the lack of legal protection afforded Burmese refugees in Thailand and survivors' associated fear of further abuse by police officers and military. Another equally pervasive factor is the inconsistent protections available to women under Thai law, reflecting traditions that favor male domination. For example, although non-marital rape is considered a serious crime under Thai law, proof of non-consent falls to the victim. This has especially devastating implications for trafficked sex workers, who are typically treated as offenders, detained, and required to pay fines and finance the expenses of their deportation.

Other Thai legal provisions generally discourage refugee women and girls from seeking protection against violence perpetrated by their host community or fellow refugee community. In cases of statutory rape, an offender may opt to marry his victim, thus avoiding punishment. Financial compensation for the rape of a married woman (by someone other than her husband) is given to the husband rather than to the survivor; the crime of marital rape does not exist, nor is the phenomenon of domestic violence formally recognized in Thai law.[13] In camp settings, more severe cases of domestic or refugee community violence against women are referred to the Burmese camp committees, which are, without exception, male dominated. Rare accounts of Burmese women successfully charging Thai military, police, or Thai civilians with sexual assault, if settled, have been according to customary compensation.[14]

## Current GBV-related Programming

Ethnic Burmese women and girls are at risk for GBV at many stages: in their home country, in flight, in the host country, and during repatriation. As such, Burmese refugees typify the experience of refugee women and girls worldwide. Even so, what was remarkable during site visits along the Thai/Burma border was not the prevalence of violence but rather its invisibility and the lack of standard GBV prevention and response activities. Although Burmese refugees have been living in Thailand some fifteen years, and accounts of sexual abuse by the Burmese military have been recorded by multiple Burmese and international human rights organizations, no camps or organizations have ongoing education, services, or protocols specifically targeting survivors of GBV. Limited activities focus on immediate protection of the victim and are the result of an isolated few international NGOs that have taken it upon themselves to establish links with local women's organizations and with UNHCR to create a network that facilitates UNHCR intervention. Nonetheless, UNHCR options for pursuing cases of GBV are restricted by the lack of protection afforded refugees by the RTG and Thai law.

### Karen Camps: NuPo and Umpiem Mai

Both NuPo and Umpiem Mai have well-developed preventive and curative primary and reproductive health services systems serving the ethnic Karen community inside the camps. Each camp also has an established network of Karen women's representatives, responsible for monitoring the needs of women and communicating those needs to the women's affairs committee and the camp council. In 1999, elected members of the women's network formed the Mae Sot-based Karen Refugee Camps Women's Development Group (KRWDG). Members of KRWDG are currently receiving skills and NGO development training in order to improve their capacity to assist women's representatives within the camps and to respond to the needs of Karen women.

In interviews with those living and working in the Karen camps, as well as with health care providers, women's representatives, and members of the KRWDG, all expressed concern about violence against women, including domestic violence, sexual assault and coercion by Thai military and Thai civilians, domestic servitude, prostitution, and forced marriage. (Notably, reports of Burmese military atrocities were missing from anecdotes of violence, which may reflect low exposure by the Karen. Most Karen living in Nu Po, for example, have been refugees for many years and were not directly subject to Burmese military aggression.) Health care providers from one international NGO designed and facilitated two trainings on general issues of violence against women and human rights, in which many of the women's representatives participated. Still, actual GBV case numbers within the camp populations are impossible to obtain and interventions—even by international and local NGOs that have articulated a real concern about GBV—appear to be ad hoc.

In NuPo camp, women's representatives respond to five to six reports of domestic violence per month, initially providing informal "education" to the couple about mutual respect, and in cases of escalating abuse, reporting the couple to the Burmese camp council. In the last several years, there have been only two instances in which the NuPo camp council placed restrictions on husbands, committing them each to camp labor and confinement for a maximum of one month. The newly assigned leader of the Umpiem Mai camp denied any knowledge of violence, deferring to the chief of the Karen Women's Organization, but nevertheless suggested that training on GBV might be worthwhile. In the recent memory of an Umpiem Mai medical worker, only one reported case of domestic violence resulted in medical treatment (there was no written record of the source of injury). One case of incest by a stepfather concluded with the perpetrator's voluntary departure from the camp. Similarly, Thai authorities resolved two cases of rape by Thai camp police by retiring one rapist and reassigning the other. Neither rape survivor, according to camp medical staff, requested or received medical follow-up. Nor have Karen women living in Umpiem Mai come forward requesting medical assistance related to Burmese military victimizations or sexual injuries incurred during flight. Although all new arrivals in Umpiem Mai receive medical exams, there is no protocol for identifying or supporting victims of GBV. In NuPo, where medical services are provided on an as-requested basis, there are also no protocols for identifying or responding to survivors of any kind of sexual assault. In both camps, rates of sexually transmitted diseases and unwanted pregnancies were reported to be low to negligible.

The existence in the last two years of UNHCR in the NuPo and Umpiem Mai camps has served a preventive function. Though UNHCR does not have a daily presence in the camps, an international camp-based NGO has facilitated links between UNHCR and the women's committees, identifying for UNHCR some of the most vulnerable women so as to help the women circumvent violence or exploitation. However, UNHCR's ability to ensure protection in identified cases of violence is unclear, as is their relationship with the local MOI authorities. For their part, MOI authorities claimed that victims of violence have access to police protection and legal assistance to the same degree as the local Thai community; yet, these same MOI authorities could recall no instances in which a refugee utilized such assistance.

## Mae Sot

The city of Mae Sot is one of several centers for trafficking across the Burmese border. With an estimated sixteen brothels and a strong textile industry, Mae Sot is often a holding ground for "illegal immigrants" crossing into Thailand.[15] Protections for non-registered refugees living in and around Mae Sot are essentially non-existent—instead, they are at fairly constant risk of summary deportation. Support services are similarly limited, with the notable exception of the Mae Tao Clinic. The most well-established and long-standing organization serving the Burmese community in Mae Sot, the clinic's free health services are provided by a large health staff that is supervised by the clinic's director, a Burmese refugee doctor whose commitment to the refugee community (and ability to win their trust as well as the cooperation of the RTG) is legendary. Recognizing the need for increased understanding of and response to issues of GBV, the clinic's director has attempted to facilitate awareness raising and psychosocial trainings for her health staff. The Mae Tao Clinic also supports women's issues by sponsoring the KRWDG and other local Burmese women's organizations. Still, there is no specific programming within the clinic targeting the medical or psychosocial needs of survivors of violence, nor is there any system for documenting violence against women. There is one organization in Mae Sot that provides safe housing for exploited sex workers, but it does not have any supportive interventions specifically addressing the effects of violence, in spite of clients such as the one described below by the organization's director:

Trafficked into prostitution at 13 years old, she worked at one of the brothels in Mae Sot that is run by a Thai and serves both Burmese and Thai men. The first time she was approached by a customer, she refused but was forced. The superintendent received a higher price for her "deflowering." As punishment for her initial resistance, she was transferred to another brothel. After several sexual relationships, she was taken by one customer and deposited in a field, where she was again raped by several men. Vomiting blood as well as bleeding from her vagina, she made her way to the roadside, where she was picked up by police who returned her to the brothel. The superintendent punished her by shackling her hands.

Given this account, it is perhaps not surprising that one of the primary concerns of refugee women seeking reproductive health services at the Mae Tao Clinic is complications related to abortions. Because abortion is illegal in both Burma and Thailand, Burmese women use traditional methods to stimulate abortions, the most alarming of which involves piercing the uterus with a sharpened stick.[16]

## Karenni Camps: Mae Hon Son Region

The Karenni National Women's Organization (KNWO) is an umbrella NGO whose members live primarily in and around three camps that provide refuge for the ethnic Karenni in Thailand's northern province of Mae Hon Son. The KNWO's mandate is to address the political and human rights of Karenni women living in Burma and in the refugee camps. In an informal focus group, representatives of KNWO roughly estimated the percentage of Karenni refugee women exposed to GBV at 60 percent. Even though this number may seem exceedingly high, it, at the very least, underscores GBV as a problem in the Karenni community. Family quarrels account for the highest percentage of violence, with rape by Burmese military and Thai civilians following second and third. Although the KNWO representatives have no documentation or formal data to confirm their impressions of the high degree of GBV encountered by Karenni refugee women, anecdotal evidence illustrates a range of violence, including sexual abuse and rape by Burmese military, rape and murder by Thai civilians, sexual abuse by Thai police, forced marriage by Thai military, rape by Karenni men inside the camps, and domestic violence. None of the cases related by the KNWO representatives resulted in prosecution of the perpetrators. Members of the KNWO, like their Karen counterparts, have participated in at least one training on issues of violence against women and human rights. Some also participated in basic training on psychosocial issues affecting survivors and were in the process of establishing a safe house for women and girls within one camp. In situations of domestic violence, the Karenni women's representatives in the camps follow the same general procedure applied by Karen women in the NuPo and Umpiem Mai camps: they address the issue directly with the couple, advising the man "not to be so hard on the woman"; if resolution of the violence is not forthcoming, the case is reported to the camp committee.

A Karenni camp committee leader asserted that domestic violence within his camp was very rare—he could only recall two or three cases within the last six years. He allowed that in domestic violence cases involving serious injury, a perpetrator might be imprisoned for three to seven days, but it was more likely that the majority of cases would be resolved within the family. Other male representatives of the camp committee concurred that physical violence between husbands and wives was a rare occurrence but suggested that verbal arguments regularly flare up because of poor economic conditions within the camp and because wives accuse their husbands of failing to provide for the family. Although requests from women for separations and divorces are high, particularly among new arrivals, the camp committee views them as passing manifestations of extreme stress and rarely grants them. Reports to the camp committee of other forms violence—committed by the Thai authorities or local Thai community—are nonexistent. Similarly, representatives of the Karenni camp Ministry of Health recalled only two or three domestic violence cases and two rape cases during their ten years of providing services. There are no established health protocols for intervening in cases of GBV. Rates of sexually transmitted diseases are low, and the Ministry of Health has received no reports of unwanted pregnancy.

## Summary

An obvious discrepancy exists between women's and human rights organizations' analyses of the extent of GBV experienced by Burmese refugees and the knowledge of GBV among other refugee representatives and service providers. This discrepancy may be the result of a heightened sensitivity to GBV issues among women advocates: Burmese women's rights organizations have proliferated within Thailand and are a major source of information about issues, including GBV, affecting Burmese women. Their accomplishments cannot be underestimated, given that restrictions imposed by the RTG severely undermine their mobility, access to resources, and ability to network with local and international women's organizations. Nevertheless, their reports of violence have not had a significant impact on GBV programming for refugee women living along the Thai/Burma border.

Another factor contributing to this discrepancy may be service providers' discomfort and lack of familiarity with GBV issues. All those interviewed had limited to no training in responding to violence against women; several expressed a desire to expand programming but felt they lacked the experience or knowledge to integrate GBV protocols into existing health and social services. Notably, two health care providers had facilitated seminars on GBV within the camps, but each expressed concerns about how to follow up. Also notable were the attempts of at least one international NGO to establish a basic system of reporting to UNHCR so that survivors could receive protective services, even if nominal.

Yet another factor is the silence about GBV that characterizes the Burmese community's response to victimization. Traditional methods of dealing with violence against women in Burmese society are executed at the family level, and public accounting results in social stigmatization. Virginity is esteemed among unmarried women, and monogamy is a mandate for married women, such that rape is a source of shame for the Burmese victim and her family. Karenni women's representatives recounted several adolescent refugees committing suicide rather than revealing their rapes by MOI officials. Legal recourse is virtually nonexistent in Burma for victims of family or state-perpetrated violence.

Likewise, given the tenuous rights of Burmese refugees, legal recourse is largely unavailable in Thailand. In many instances reporting may increase a refugee's risk of exploitation and forced repatriation. The MOI, border patrol, and Thai military appear to enjoy relative impunity in cases of sexual violence against refugees, and the laws within Thailand favor patriarchal traditions. UNHCR, international, and local NGOs working with refugees must comply with the regulations and practices of the RTG, a delicate position from which to advocate for GBV survivors' rights if violations are committed by representatives of the RTG.

Additional challenges to designing and implementing GBV services for Burmese refugees include the diversity of ethnic groups represented, variations in exposure to violence in Burma, and variations in exposure to violence in Thailand. The range of traditions and experience represented by the Burmese refugees—as well as the environmental differences among refugees living in camps compared to those absorbed into cities such as Mae Sot—requires creative and highly adaptive GBV interventions.

In spite of the difficulties of addressing GBV among refugees living along the Thai/Burma border, there are existing resources within Thailand that may be exploited to develop programming. The first is the network of refugee women's organizations; each expressed an interest in expanding their knowledge and resources regarding GBV. UNHCR and international NGOs working in the camps similarly appeared interested in developing more concrete programming for refugee survivors. International and Thai women's organizations, mostly based in larger cities such as Bangkok and Chiang Mai, may be able to contribute their expertise to service providers working in camps.

Thailand and Burma are both signatories of CEDAW and thus have formally committed to improve the conditions of women. In February 2000 the two countries' ministries of health agreed to combat health problems along the Thai/Burma border.[17] This spirit of cooperation may provide one portal for advancing programming for GBV, both in Thailand and Burma, and allow for the adoption of legislation that addresses all forms of GBV, especially domestic violence and forced prostitution.

## Recommendations

1.  The RTG should develop a specific policy outlining a code of conduct for government security and police representatives working with refugees—including MOI, military, and border patrols—and institute mechanisms for enforcing that policy. Severe penalties should be levied for any members of the Thai security forces, or the Thai community in general, who participate in forced prostitution, or in any other way support the sexual exploitation and assault of Burmese women and girls.

2.  The RTG should work with UNHCR in establishing systems of confidential reporting for cases of GBV so as to ensure refugees the right to safety and security. It should also establish mechanisms for prosecution of GBV crimes should the survivors seek prosecution.

3.  UNHCR should provide training to all refugee communities on basic refugee rights, including legal recourse in cases of GBV committed by fellow refugees or the host community.

4.  Members of the BBC should establish strategies to address GBV throughout refugee camps in Thailand, with specific provisions for: 1) accommodating the needs of culturally diverse refugee populations; 2) creating a sectoral response that identifies paths of intervention for health, psychosocial, education, and security sectors; and 3) coordination among the sectors and with representatives of the women's committees and the camp councils. The strategies should be designed with the full and ongoing participation of all involved in their implementation, with priority attention given to members of the refugee community, especially camp leadership structures and women's committees.

5.  For the health sector, strategies should include: methods of confidential and active screening for health providers; conducting rape exams; and collecting and monitoring GBV-related health data. For the psychosocial sector (largely comprised of women's committees) strategies should include: supportive interventions for survivors; creating safe spaces for survivors; establishing links with other sectors; and conducting basic education in the community about GBV-related issues and services. For the education sector, strategies should include sensitization curricula (that may be implemented by youth organizations) introducing basic education to adolescents about healthy relationships, safe touch, and

access to assistance. For the security sector (including UNHCR protection officers and MOI officials) strategies should include methods of immediate assistance, police reporting, referrals for prosecution, data collection, and coordination.

6. Trainings to introduce the strategies should engage the expertise of GBV-related Thai and Burmese organizations in Chiang Mai and Bangkok and should be based on a training of trainers model in which Burmese women and men can provide ongoing trainings to members of their communities.

7. UNHCR, MOI, and the BBC should be responsible for ongoing oversight of implementation of strategies and for coordination of GBV-related activities and data collection. Mechanisms should be introduced to regularly evaluate data and adjust programming accordingly. Data should also be used to conduct ongoing advocacy and facilitate communication with the RTG about the nature and scope of GBV among the refugee population.

8. UNHCR should facilitate ongoing participatory education campaigns targeting refugees living outside of the camps on issues of GBV. UNHCR should also solidify links with health and other organizations providing services to non-camp refugees and support those organizations' capacity to address GBV.

## Notes

1   Women's Commission for Refugee Women and Children, *Fear and Hope: Displaced Burmese Women in Burma and Thailand* (New York, 2000), 3.

2   Images Asia, *Alternative Perspectives, Other Voices: Assessing Gender Equality in Burma* (Bangkok, 1999), 2.

3   Memorandum, Burmese Border Consortium (BBC), *Refugee Population Figures* (Bangkok, 2000), 1.

4   BBC, *Program Report for January-June 2000* (Bangkok 2000), ii.

5   Images Asia, *Alternative Perspectives, Other Voices*, 3.

6   B. Apple, *School for Rape: The Burmese Military and Sexual Violence*, EarthRights International (Bangkok, 1998), 13.

7   *Equality, Development and Peace for Women: National Report;* cited in, Images Asia, *Alternative Perspectives, Other Voices*, 1.

8   Images Asia, *Alternative Perspectives, Other Voices*, 27.

9   National Coalition Government of the Union of Burma, *Burma: The Current State of Women—Conflict Area Specific* (Bangkok, 2000), 27.

10  Images Asia, *Alternative Perspectives, Other Voices*, 28.

11  Human Rights Documentation Unit and Burmese Women's Union, *Cycle of Suffering* (Bangkok, 2000), 10.

12  See the monthly newsletters of the Burmese Women's Union, accessible on-line at www.freeburma.org.

13  World Organization Against Torture, *Violence Against Women in Thailand* (Geneva, 1998), 15.

14  Images Asia, *Alternative Perspectives, Other Voices*, 70.

15  Burmese Women's Union, *Cycle of Suffering* (Bangkok, 2000), 46.

16  Burmese Women's Union, *Cycle of Suffering*, 81.

17  Mae Tao Clinic, *Annual Report 2000* (Mae Sot 2001), 10.

# Post-conflict Situation in *East Timor*

May 7-14, 2001

## Background

### Historical Context

Following its 1975 invasion and unlawful annexing of East Timor, Indonesia occupied the small half-island with a military iron fist, and for almost twenty-five years committed well-documented human rights abuses in its mission to suppress virtually all aspects of East Timorese society. With rare exception, the accounts of ongoing torture, extra-judicial executions, rapes, and disappearances were largely ignored by the international community, until the 1996 Nobel Peace Prize was awarded to two East Timorese rights advocates: José Ramos-Horta and Bishop Carlos Belo. As violence escalated throughout Indonesia, internal and international pressure facilitated the end of Indonesian President Suharto's thirty-two-year reign, and in 1998 Suharto's "adopted son," B. J. Habibie, inherited the presidential mantle. Promising reforms, President Habibie signed an agreement allowing the United Nations to conduct a 1999 ballot referendum on establishing East Timor as an autonomous state within Indonesia. Against a rising wave of violent militia-based intimidation, nearly 80 percent of the East Timorese population turned out to vote, overwhelmingly casting their ballots in favor of independence.[1]

Immediately after the announcement of the referendum's results, pro-Indonesian militia groups across East Timor launched a reprisal campaign of systematic destruction. U.N. personnel were driven out of East Timor, most cities were razed, and mass deaths, disap-

pearances, and displacement went unchecked by the Indonesian military and government. Several hundred thousand East Timorese were relocated at gunpoint to camps in West Timor, and hundreds of thousands more sought refuge in East Timor's hills until Habibie, relenting to international pressure, allowed peace-keeping forces to enter East Timor and quell the violence. On October 20, 1999, Habibie was defeated in a democratic election by Abdurrahman Wahid, whose stated commitment to human rights and Indonesian democratization elicited the provisional support of the international community.

### Current Government

The U.N. established a Transitional Administration in East Timor (UNTAET), whose original protectorate function amounted to almost absolute control over establishing East Timor's basic institutions. UNTAET and the National Council of East Timor Resistance have since shifted to a coalition government referred to as the East Timor Transitional Administration (ETTA), with eight ministries responsible for developing East Timor's infrastructure. A gender representative has been designated within the Social Affairs Ministry to assist women's organizations, but because her position provides community support and not government oversight, she has limited ability to influence government structure and policy. Government advocacy has been a primary concern of the U.N.'s Gender Affairs Unit, which has deployed gender representatives to each of East Timor's districts in order to gain field-level insights about issues affecting women. Despite its broad reach, the Gender Affairs Unit is marginal to the government structure, and at present there is no provision for the Unit's inclusion in East Timor's permanent government.

## Status of Women

Indonesian law is currently the applicable standard, modified in order to meet international codes, which the U.N.-administered civilian police (CIVPOL) are meant to enforce. As outlined below, Indonesian law explicitly favors the subordination of women, limiting CIVPOL's ability to intervene on behalf of East Timorese women. However, CIVPOL has taken the lead in responding to reports of violence. In one example illustrative of the tradition of violent discrimination against women, a husband who had recently beaten his wife tried to have CIVPOL arrest her for disobedience and was dismayed when CIVPOL arrested him instead. Yet even in cases of violence against women, CIVPOL has limited reach; its Vulnerable Persons Unit (VPU)—the arm responsible for investigating sensitive cases such as sexual assault and domestic violence—is currently only operating in the capital, Dili, because of the lack of expert personnel. Their limited reach is especially alarming given the apparent rates of violence: between July and December 2000, over 260 cases of domestic violence and sexual assault were reported to the Dili Police Unit.[2]

In the absence of strong national programming, several international donor agencies and international and local women's NGOs have taken on the task of advocating for women's rights to equality. They have been especially critical in publicizing, declaiming, and responding to GBV against East Timorese women and girls.

## Gender-based Violence

Gender equality in East Timor—or, rather, its absence—has largely been informed by traditional patriarchal customs reinforced by Indonesian law and practice. Although Indonesia ratified the United Nations Convention on the Elimination of All Forms of Discrimination Against Women (CEDAW) in 1984 and actively participated in the Beijing Conference on Women in 1995, polygamy, male domination within the family, and divorce rights favoring men are explicitly supported within Indonesian law.[3] Because

they are not formally recognized within the law as violations of women's rights, marital rape, dowry-related exploitation, and other traditional forms of violence against women receive de facto reinforcement.[4] Domestic and community violence, as well as the trafficking of women and girls, are addressed within Indonesia's penal code, yet generally go unreported and unprosecuted because of prevailing mores that stigmatize victims and relegate violence against women to the private sphere, where it remains unresolved, or is traditionally redressed through remuneration to the victim's family.[5] State-perpetrated violence, also recognized in Indonesia's penal code, was reportedly carried out with impunity by Indonesian troops against East Timorese women.[6]

## During Conflict

During Indonesian occupation of East Timor, women were subject to the same types of intimidation, arbitrary arrest, detention, torture, and killing as their male counterparts. Women and girls were additionally exposed to GBV, including violations of reproductive rights (forced or coerced contraception), rape, sexual harassment, enforced slavery, and forced or coerced prostitution servicing Indonesian military troops.[7] Women with an assumed relationship to Falintil, the East Timorese resistance movement, were particular targets for state-sanctioned and perpetrated sexual abuses.[8] Those living in rural areas were at greater risk of enforced slavery and prostitution as a result of their isolation, lack of education, and economic disempowerment.[9] The presence of the military also contributed to a flourishing and well-organized sex industry in East Timor. Although that industry has become more fragmented since the military's departure, it is nevertheless still active, according to an expatriate doctor who suspects that the increase in sexually transmitted infections among his female patients is the result of prostitution.

In the violence and chaos ensuing from the 1999 referendum, militia groups reportedly carried on the Indonesian military's practice of sexual crimes against women, systematically raping women, sometimes in the presence of family members, or forcibly transporting women across the border into West Timor to serve as sex slaves, where thousands are estimated to remain.[10] According to the findings of the U.N. Special Rapporteur on Violence Against Women, the Indonesian military command both implicitly and explicitly supported these crimes.[11]

The U.N. was reputedly slow and clumsy—failing to use female interviewers and ensure confidentiality—in its preliminary investigations of war crimes involving GBV. Nor did the initial report of the United Nations High Commissioner for Refugees (UNHCR) include provisions for a just and rapid response to women victims, such as appropriate investigation into reported cases or efforts to detain and return (primarily from West Timor) suspected perpetrators.[12] However, women's organizations existing before the 1999 siege quickly regrouped—a remarkable feat given that they had only come into formal existence after Suharto's departure in 1998. With financial support and technical assistance from a boom of international donors and NGOs, these women's organizations started responding to GBV survivors. From late 1999 through the end of 2000, the Communication Forum for East Timorese Women (FOKUPERS) identified and assisted 182 women and children survivors of siege-related violence in East Timor's thirteen districts[13]; and the East Timorese Women Against Violence (ET-WAVE) identified and worked with another 232 survivors of militia and military-based sexual abuse perpetrated before and during the siege.[14]

## Beyond Conflict

Among those organizations supporting women, the initial focus on survivors of political violence rapidly expanded to embrace other forms of GBV, particularly domestic violence, which was perceived by East Timorese women's representatives to have escalated after the referendum as a result of stress, unemployment, and dislocation. Pre-existing and burgeoning local women's organizations agreed in early 2000 to form the East Timorese Women's Network (REDE), and in June 2000 convened the first Congress of Women of Timor Loro Sae (East Timor). There they drafted a comprehensive platform of action that identified as one area of critical concern a pervasive East Timorese "culture of violence" resulting from the legacy of occupation. Other highlighted problems relating to GBV included spousal abuse, polygamy, marital rape, incest, violence against women in the workplace and school, and bride price and other inheritance inequities. Among the platform's calls for action was the right of women survivors of Indonesian atrocities to seek justice through an international tribunal; improved protection and services for survivors of community and domestic

violence; revisions of laws that currently enforce women's subordinate status; and mass education about women's rights.[15]

## Current GBV-related Programming

Although it has a long way to go before responding to all the concerns outlined in the platform of action of the Women's Congress, East Timor in many ways exemplifies the advances in programming women can make when gender issues are granted even marginal local, national, or international support. The following is a partial representation of activities currently underway in East Timor's capital city of Dili to prevent and respond to GBV. Notably, all have been initiated only in the last several years, and few have operations that extend to other of East Timor's thirteen districts.

### Dili: Local Initiatives

The most prominent Dili-based local organizations working on GBV are FOKUPERS and ET-WAVE. Both have dramatically expanded their scope of activity since receiving post-independence support from multiple international organizations. FOKUPERS's broad objectives are threefold: 1) case management and practical assistance throughout East Timor to women and children survivors of Indonesian and family violence; 2) advocacy regarding survivor and general women's issues; and 3) education and training on human rights with a special orientation toward women's and children's rights. Specific FOKUPERS activities include running a safe house in Dili for victims of violence; legal and economic support to survivors; family mediation in cases of domestic violence; and radio and print media campaigns. ET-WAVE's program has similar objectives and activities. They run a safe house in Ermera District and provide services to women in various districts, including counseling, literacy, and small business funding to survivors of Indonesian and domestic violence.

FOKUPERS and ET-WAVE are also part of a rape response team, along with the Young Women's Groups from East Timor (GFFTL), which is coordinating a 24-hour safe room for rape survivors based out of Dili Hospital. The International Rescue Committee (IRC) has taken the lead in organizing the response team and in building its capacity to provide counseling and case management services for an average of three to five safe room clients per month. Aside from working on the safe room team, GFFTL has conducted awareness-raising sessions among young women and girls on gender, sexuality, and GBV. The East Timor Commission for Human Rights (CDHTL), a newly developed local NGO, has been trained and financially supported by IRC to provide GBV seminars and investigate abuses of women in districts outside of Dili.

The Timorese Women's Organization (OMT), a politically non-aligned offshoot of the East Timorese women's resistance movement, has not yet developed any activities specific to GBV, but through its countrywide networks it has facilitated data collection on vulnerable women and children for UNTAET. OMT also assisted IRC in conducting focus groups on women's rights and will be supported by IRC to deliver the results of the assessment to participants. Similarly, the Association of Women Jurists (ANEMTIL) has not focused overtly on GBV, but it has worked closely with the Gender Affairs Unit to establish a gender and law group that will be well-positioned to influence draft legislation on the prevention of and response to GBV.

As the coordinating body of the local East Timor women's organizations, REDE's objectives include information sharing, policy development, and advocacy on women's issues. It is currently composed of fifteen member organizations, including those mentioned above. Other organizations such as Timor Aid, Prontu Atu Serbi (PAS), Hermanas Carmelitas, AMST, and HOTFILMA are providing a range of health, economic, and social services that target vulnerable women and children.

## Dili: International
## Non-Governmental Initiatives

A number of international NGOs that entered East Timor following the referendum have provided technical assistance to local women's organizations on issues ranging from political and gender-based community education to NGO administration and micro-enterprise programming, but only three INGOs have focused on GBV. Caritas-Australia recently initiated six months of training for FOKUPERS and ET-WAVE on sexual assault response skills, police and court procedures, and victims' rights. The Program for Psychosocial Recovery and Development in East Timor has provided a one-time

psychosocial training and ongoing information to FOKUPERS, ET-WAVE, churches, and schools in issues of domestic and sexual violence. Although the contributions of these international NGOs have been significant, neither has programs that focus exclusively on issues of violence. The longest-running and most-specialized international program addressing GBV has been facilitated by IRC.

In early 2000, IRC collaborated with OMT, ET-WAVE, GFFTL, and CDHTL to conduct a series of focus groups on women's rights in five target districts, where—anticipating the concerns later identified at East Timor's first Women's Congress—participants variously identified marital violence (including forced sex), family violence (particularly abuse from brothers), polygamy, dowry-based oppression, unequal access to education, and sexual harassment as points of concern. IRC followed this assessment with a broad-based GBV capacity building program whose objectives include providing ongoing coordination of and support to local NGOs that already conduct or wish to undertake GBV-related activities. IRC facilitated the Dili hospital safe room and response team, provided NGO training of trainers on GBV, distributed small-scale financing for GBV outreach activities to organizations in multiple districts, and coordinated and funded an exchange trip for East Timorese women's representatives to Australia, where they met with several organizations addressing GBV in Australia's northern territory. Otherwise notable among IRC's activities were an in-house training on sexual harassment to IRC employees; participatory design and dissemination of multi-media GBV awareness-raising resources; coordination with CIVPOL's VPU on GBV referral procedures; and successful advocacy with the VPU that resulted in sex-disaggregated data on assaults (which currently outnumber all other reported crimes).

## Dili: United Nations and
## Government Initiatives

A community services representative at UNHCR with expertise in GBV has worked closely with CIVPOL's VPU to improve police response to GBV survivors, taking the exemplary initiative to develop and conduct training for East Timorese police cadets on investigation techniques, attitudes toward GBV, health services for survivors, women's organizations, conducting child interviews, and so forth. UNHCR has also implemented programs for West Timor returnees through ET-WAVE and FOKUPERS, providing each organization with infrastructural and financial support. The United Nations Development Fund for Women (UNIFEM) is supplying a permanent secretariat for REDE as well as administrative capacity building for REDE staff. The Dili District Administration Gender Office has assisted REDE in coordinating special events, including "16 Days of Activism Against Gender-based Violence," and is co-chairing with REDE four women's affairs committees. The Gender Office has also published a resource listing of women's organizations in Dili, with a useful bibliography of reference materials on general women's issues available for reprint or loan from organizations in Dili. Under the advisement of the ETTA Gender Affairs Unit, the Gender Office also conducted a survey of East Timorese women who had achieved post-secondary high school education—8 percent of the 660 women surveyed—in order to facilitate women's inclusion in civil service by identifying potential candidates. Most notable, the Gender Affairs Unit has recently collaborated with the United Nations Population Fund (UNFPA) to develop a comprehensive nationwide project on GBV in order to collect secondary data (types, prevalence, consequences, existing services); formulate preventive and protective legislation; conduct advocacy and education activities; and establish coordinated community services (among health providers, social services, judiciary, police, and women's advocates) for the prevention of and response to GBV.

## Summary

The comprehensive objectives of the ETTA/UNFPA project are timely. As the programming above suggests, local and international organizations have made a commitment to addressing GBV in East Timor. Some of the most remarkable activities include FOKUPERS and ET-WAVE's rapid response to survivors of Indonesian violence and subsequent attention to domestic violence, the first Women's Congress and resulting Platform for Action, UNHCR's direct investment in police training on GBV, Dili Hospital's safe room, IRC's community-based capacity-building model, and the sex-disaggregated data analysis system of CIVPOL's VPU. Even so, according to those interviewed, most initiatives are limited in scope, temporary, or do not yet have nationwide relevance.

The VPU, for example, currently exists only in Dili, and its investment in GBV is largely a result of the (temporary) presence of expatriates with experience policing GBV. The Dili Hospital's safe room is the only one of its kind throughout East Timor, and the Department of Health Services has no plans to integrate GBV into its national rehabilitation and development program—in spite of one doctor claiming that his top priority would be to establish health clinics for vulnerable women. There are no national government programs or ministries addressing violence against women, and the U.N.'s Gender Affairs Unit anticipates being dislocated from the national government structure before national elections in 2002.

The UNHCR representative committed to supporting GBV programs and police training is unique within UNHCR East Timor. Her activities reflect her personal expertise and interest more than an institutionalized commitment within East Timor's UNHCR offices to addressing GBV. Although there is a women jurists' association (ANEMTIL), all fifteen public defenders in East Timor are men, and traditional justice works against women. In a representative case, a man who claimed that he repeatedly digitally raped his wife's fourteen-year-old sister "by accident" was released and returned home, where he subsequently paid his wife's family five buffalo to settle the matter.

Many U.N. organizations, including the Gender Affairs Unit, have been slow to hire East Timorese for substantive positions, such that capacity building for women has been mostly limited to small-scale local programs and enterprises. (This is in part attributable to the long history of limited education afforded women and girls and the resulting high illiteracy rates, which are being met with large-scale literacy programs and improved schooling.) Most of East Timor's GBV-focused organizations are Dili-based, and therefore have limited impact in other towns or outlying areas.

Moreover, local and international representatives identified several challenges to existing programs. For example, FOKUPERS and ET-WAVE are relatively new NGOs—indeed East Timor's entire civil sector is new—and are still in the process of developing their missions. This task has been complicated by the numerous international NGOs attempting to assist them and has resulted in a diversification in programming that may undermine their effectiveness in addressing GBV. Similarly, REDE has received support from several international sources, but it has yet to realize its potential as a coordinating and advocacy organization and must contend with inevitable competition from local member NGOs for finite international resources. Although social services existed during the Indonesian occupation, none focused on supportive interventions for women; counseling skills are a relatively new acquisition of the women's groups. The short-term counselor trainings they have had are insufficient to build their full capacity, and the lack of ongoing supervision has resulted in counselors relying on traditional means of giving advice. One counselor reported that she typically tells the survivors with whom she works to "try and forget."

Other aspects of GBV programming are altogether absent in East Timor. An ideal continuum of GBV post-conflict response would begin at the border as returnees cross from West Timor, where GBV survivors would be identified and provided immediate support services. At present, no such services exist (nor are they provided within West Timor, given the unstable security). No central organization has taken the lead in collecting current countrywide statistics on GBV, and there is no national mandate for submitting such data. Only a handful of organizations or institutions have methods for capturing and analyzing GBV data. There are no nationwide education campaigns on various types of GBV, and no clinic-based educational materials. Apparently no programs exist for sex workers, though there was a well-organized brothel system during Indonesian occupation, and an ongoing informal network of prostitutes, some of whom are transported from Jakarta and Portugal, is still active. There are no support programs for male survivors, in spite of testimony by female survivors that East Timorese men were forced by the Indonesian military to commit rapes.

The scope of the ETTA/UNFPA project has the promise of casting GBV issues under a brighter spotlight, thus stimulating existing and future prevention and response activities. And yet, without the support of government institutions committed to integrating GBV concerns into their institutional mandates, issues of GBV will continue to be the peripheral reserve of small-scale programs.

## Recommendations

1. The U.N.'s Gender Affairs Unit should be institutionalized within East Timor's permanent government. The Gender Affairs Unit or its equivalent should be charged with facilitating coordination of multisectoral GBV activities. The model of locally based gender affairs officers should continue under the new government, and those officers should be responsible for monitoring and advising local efforts to address GBV.

2. The health, social services, judicial, and police systems must work to improve their understanding of and coordinated response to GBV, particularly as new legislation is drafted. Ministries responsible for overseeing health, social services, and law enforcement should each mandate data collection and analysis in their respective sectors. The data should be used to facilitate training of personnel and improve intersectoral accountability. Each sector should have specific and standardized protocols for addressing survivor needs.

3. The government should support broad-based, multi-media community education on issues of GBV. Specific campaigns should be introduced to target specific populations and GBV issues. Standard education programs about conflict resolution and healthy relationships should be introduced in the schools.

4. International donors and implementing organizations should continue to financially and technically support women's organizations to implement GBV programming, with special considerations for developing these programs from the emergency post-conflict phase into long-term sustainable development projects. Special consideration should also be given to expanding current Dili-based programming throughout East Timor.

5. Local coordinating bodies such as REDE should develop a GBV task force whose responsibilities include national advocacy as well as monitoring and supporting field-based activities.

6. Initiatives such as IRC's, which have facilitated education of Timorese GBV organizations by experts in Australia, should be expanded so that

local NGO representatives have access to international training and forums.

7.  Men, often the most marginalized within GBV programming, should be integrated into all prevention activities. Programs for male survivors of sexual violence perpetrated during the Indonesian occupation should be implemented throughout East Timor.

## Notes

1   East Timor Human Rights Center, *The Right to Be Heard: Documenting Human Rights Violations for Justice* (Melbourne, 1999), 1.

2   International Rescue Committee, "Common Goals, Different Roles: Discussion from Sector-specific Focus Groups on Sexual and Gender-based Violence in East Timor" (unpublished report, Dili, 2001), 3.

3   World Organization Against Torture (OMCT), *Violence Against Women in East Timor: Report Prepared for the Committee on the Elimination of Discrimination Against Women* (Geneva, 1998), 17-19.

4   OMCT, *Violence Against Women in East Timor*, 20-22.

5   OMCT, *Violence Against Women in East Timor*, 20, 23, 28.

6   See East Timor Human Rights Center, *Violence by the State Against Women in East Timor: A Report to the U.N. Special Rapporteur on Violence Against Women* (Melbourne, 1997).

7   M. Sissons, *From One Day to Another: Violations of Women's Reproductive Rights in East Timor* (report for East Timor Human Rights Center, Dili, 1997); see also, Kiyoko Furusawa and Jean Inglis, "Violence Against Women in East Timor Under the Indonesian Occupation," in Lourdes Sojor, ed., *Common Grounds* (Philippines, 1998), 293-300.

8   United Nations, Special Rapporteur on Violence Against Women, *Mission to Indonesia and East Timor* (Geneva, 1998), 17.

9   Sissons, *From One Day to Another*, 31-32.

10  S. Powell, "Rape: Just Another Weapon of War," *Weekend Australian*, 20 March 2001, 20.

11  U.S. Department of State, *Country Report on Human Rights Practices: East Timor* (Washington, D.C., 2000), 2.

12  Human Rights Watch, *Human Rights Watch World Report 2001* (New York, 2001).

13  FOKUPERS, "Rehabilitation Program Final Report" (unpublished report, Dili, November 1999-May 2000), 3.

14  United Nations Population Fund, "East Timor and Gender-based Violence: Project Agreement between East Timor Transitional Administration and the United Nations Population Fund" (unpublished document, Dili, May 2001), 5.

15  East Timorese Women's Network, "Statement of the first Congress of Women of Timor Loro Sae" (unpublished document, Dili, June 2000).

Country Profiles from
Eastern Europe

*Azerbaijan*
*Bosnia and Herzegovina*
*Kosovo*

# Refugees and Internally Displaced in *Azerbaijan*

June 3-10, 2001

## Background

### Historical Context

The dove-shaped land mass that forms contemporary Azerbaijan has been carved, paradoxically, from centuries of battle over this east-west trading route. At the end of World War I, Azerbaijan seized an opportunity for independence from its occupying neighbors, Russia to the north and Iran to the south. The newly declared Democratic Republic of Azerbaijan was short-lived, however. Following an invasion by Bolshevik army units in 1920, the Soviet Union forcibly incorporated Azerbaijan in 1922. While under Soviet control, a vertical swath of Azerbaijan was ceded by the Soviets to its Armenian state, geographically isolating the area of Nakhchivan from the rest of Azerbaijan, and stimulating border tensions between Armenia and Azerbaijan. In the late 1980s Armenia escalated activities to lay claim to Nagorno-Karabakh, an ethnically mixed region in western Azerbaijan adjacent to Armenia. To the dismay of Azerbaijan, Armenia's 1990 declaration on sovereignty identified Nagorno-Karabakh as its territory. Thus, even as Azerbaijan achieved its long-anticipated independence from the former USSR in 1991, the country found itself embroiled in yet another conflict.

Reaching its peak from 1988 until a 1994 cease-fire, the border war precipitated the flight of Azeris from Armenia, Nagorno-Karabakh, and surrounding areas, as well as an exodus of Armenians from Azerbaijan. Some Azeris are reportedly still being held in Armenia: the Azerbaijan Commission for Military Hostages and Captives estimates that over four hundred women and children are among those forcibly detained.[1] Though armed skirmishes have waned, Armenian forces and forces of the self-proclaimed Republic of Nagorno-Karabakh continue to occupy 20 percent of Azerbaijan territory. Tensions resulting from the unresolved conflict contribute to the challenges of securing democracy in Azerbaijan. (President Heydar Aliyev assumed power following the 1993 overthrow of his popularly elected predecessor and in 1998 retained his presidency in a controversial re-election. The current parliament, though multiparty, is dominated by Aliyev's supporters.)

### Situation of Refugees and Internally Displaced

Approximately 800,000 refugees and internally displaced persons (IDPs) are scattered in makeshift urban settlements or rural camps throughout Azerbaijan. As Azerbaijan counts on rich petroleum reserves and agricultural potential to secure its competitive future in the global market, the territorial dispute and its drain of government resources has cast a ten-year shadow over the country's transition to independence. The Organization for Security and Cooperation in Europe (OSCE) recently assumed responsibility for assisting in Nagorno-Karabakh negotiations. Even so, resolution and return of refugees and IDPs do not appear imminent. In a further crisis, the year 2000 saw some seven thousand Chechens join the ranks of Azerbaijan's refugees. Despite government reports suggesting that the economy is on the upswing (manifested especially in the growing urban business class), the average per capita income is an estimated $500/year.[2] According to the World Bank, 60 percent of Azerbaijan citizens live in poverty.[3] Among those most affected are the unemployed majority within refugee and IDP populations. Not surprising, women and children are at greatest risk.

## Status of Women

The contracting horizons of women refugees and IDPs are all the more discouraging given their high levels of literacy, education, and professional capacity: in some settlements and camps, the unemployment rate among women approaches 80 percent even though over a third of displaced adult females have specialized degrees and/or training.[4] Perhaps even worse, encamped girls may not enjoy the same access to education that defined their mother's generation. According to a United Nations Development Program (UNDP) report, there has been a significant increase in the camps of girls withdrawing from school after they complete primary grades.[5]

To a certain extent, these latest disadvantages for women and girls are an extension of long-standing patriarchal traditions. Though Soviet rule supported girls' education and allowed for a working women's proletariat, women throughout Azerbaijan are typically underemployed, averaging wage rates 51 to 84 percent lower than their male counterparts.[6] And though current laws allow for broad-based equal rights among the sexes, custom favors male leadership in both public and private spheres. Of the 125 members of the current parliament, eleven are women, and only two women direct ministries.[7] A declining but existent practice of family voting permits men to cast ballots for their female family members.[8] The constitution allows for marriage contracts on the basis of mutual consent, yet arranged marriages in which wives are incorporated into their spouse's family are reportedly still prevalent in rural areas, and traditions prescribe family authority to husbands.[9] Although Azerbaijan has a strong culture of family reverence and mutual spousal respect, several women's organizations believe GBV to be endemic. However, revelations by survivors are inhibited by cultural taboos—one estimate places reports of domestic violence at 10 percent of the total number of cases.[10]

Both despite and because of cultural traditions, international, governmental, and local advocates are working to ensure that women's rights and gender issues receive adequate attention in the government's and civil sector's evolving agendas. Since the beginning of the Azerbaijan Republic, an estimated forty-four women's NGOs have formally registered.[11] In 1995 Azerbaijan signed the United Nations Convention on the Elimination of All Forms of Discrimination Against Women (CEDAW); in 1997 UNDP initiated a comprehensive four-year Gender in Development (GID) project to support governmental institutionalization of gender planning and monitoring; in 1998 a presidential decree established the State Committee on Women's Issues (SCWI) to formulate gender-sensitive policies and programs; and in 2000 the Open Society Institute (OSI) and OSCE also incorporated gender concerns into their programming in Azerbaijan.[12] Despite this progressive orientation to gender issues, few organizations have initiatives to address the issue of GBV.

## Gender-based Violence

### During Conflict

There appears to be no documentation—anecdotal or otherwise—of violence that Azeri women or Armenian women living in Azerbaijan experienced during the height of the Nagorno-Karabakh war, though some IDP women have informally acknowledged that rapes were committed by Armenian soldiers during the conflict. Nor are data available about the abuses to which Azeri women currently held hostage in Armenia may be exposed.

### Beyond Conflict

The limited statistics about GBV in Azerbaijan have been collected only recently, and those which exist focus on general exposure rather than war-related incidents. In 1998 the local women's NGO Symmetry, with funding and technical support from UNDP's GID project, undertook the first-ever survey on domestic violence against Azeri women, which found that 37 percent of women interviewed in four regions of Azerbaijan had been subject to violent family conflict.[13] On the heels of Symmetry's research, the Azerbaijan Women's Development Center (AWDC), supported by the United Nations

Development Fund for Women (UNIFEM), surveyed eleven districts in the capital city Baku. The report on findings identifies sisters-in-law and mothers-in-law, as well as husbands, as perpetrators of violence. The report further contends that violence is related to poverty, and that women who possess their own property are less vulnerable to family violence. Although data comparing refugees and IDPs with non-refugees and non-IDPs were not teased from Symmetry's or AWDC's research, this last finding suggests that refugee and IDP women may be among the most likely victims, given their generally low economic status and lack of property.[14]

A study undertaken in 2000 by the Centers for Disease Control (CDC) and Relief International confirms this assumption. Initial results indicate that of 701 women surveyed, 25 percent had been forced to have sex (perpetrators unidentified) at some point in their life. Refugee and IDP women were at greater risk for forced sex than non-refugee and non-IDP women.[15] A subsequent study by Pathfinder International and the Azerbaijan Sociological Association exclusively analyzed refugee and IDP women and found that 23 percent of women interviewed had been beaten by their husbands. Almost 10 percent reported they had been beaten two to three times in the month prior to the interview, and 10 percent had been beaten four or more times; of the remaining, 51 percent said they were not beaten, but a significant 26 percent did not wish to respond to the question.[16]

Stigma attached to reporting is surely one determinant of the high level of non-response to the Pathfinder investigation on domestic violence. Even if Azerbaijani women were to report, they would have little legal recourse or protection. No government-based programs exist to support survivors, and non-governmental programming is severely limited in geographic and programmatic reach. Although a law was recently passed declaring spousal rape a crime, no specific laws exist to protect women from other types of spousal abuse. And while rape of any kind is considered a serious crime, incidents are rarely prosecuted: official national statistics for 2000 reveal only forty-four reported cases.[17] Few of the most vulnerable women seek medical help for gynecological problems that may arise from their victimization: over 67 percent of refugee and IDP women surveyed by Pathfinder had never visited a gynecologist, and over 75 percent did not know the meaning of "repro-

ductive health."[18] If women were to reveal a sexual assault to their gynecologist, the doctor is compelled by law to report the case—another possible contributor to low numbers of survivors seeking help.

In this climate of limited protective services, economic despair, and silence regarding violence against women, other forms of GBV have apparently burgeoned. Participants at a 1999 conference on prostitution facilitated by the Society for the Defense of Women's Rights (SDWR) asserted that Baku was home to some thirty brothels, stimulating a very active campaign by the mayor to introduce a curfew on restaurants to decrease local nightlife.[19] A field-based International Rescue Committee (IRC) health worker educating men about sexually transmitted infections (STIs) began targeting prostitutes for education after realizing that the growing sex industry in communities surrounding IDP camps in the western region of Azerbaijan was a potential source for the rapid spread of STIs.[20] Because national statistics on rates of HIV infection are extremely limited, it is difficult to determine whether the recent rise in reported HIV cases is the result of increased attention to the issue or increased rates of transmission. In any case, only two new cases of HIV infection were reported in 1996, whereas over seventy cases were reported in 1999.[21]

Although organized sex solicitation is illegal, sex transactions are considered a personal exchange and therefore outside the realm of prosecution. The laws on trafficking, however, have recently been revised to reflect concern about Azerbaijan's growing sex trade, so that forced prostitution now carries a ten- to fifteen-year sentence. Azerbaijan is reportedly a source and transit point for trafficked women en route primarily to Europe and the United Arab Emirates, as well as Saudi Arabia.[22] A preliminary investigation of trafficking by the International Organization for Migration (IOM), the leading organization worldwide in responding to and preventing sex trafficking of women, identified advertisements in local Azeri newspapers offering work abroad to "pretty girls." One, for example, solicited "tall, pretty, English-speaking girls to apply as translators in the Netherlands—knowledge of the Dutch language not required."[23] Although undoubtedly some women freely choose to work in the sex industry, the findings of IRC, IOM, and representatives of local organizations suggest that women are often either forced into sex work because of economic circumstances or they are duped by false pretenses into being trafficked—or both.

## Current GBV-related Programming

However preliminary the above-referenced studies, they confirm that domestic violence, sexual violence, prostitution, and trafficking exist in Azerbaijan. And yet, among refugee and IDP communities, where the high percentage of single women and scarcity of resources would seem to make women and girls all the more vulnerable to abuse, there is no programming to address GBV. In fact, the overall decline in funding for IDP populations has resulted in a commensurate waning of some of the most basic health and humanitarian services. Contraception, for example, was once available for free in health centers in the camps, but in a transition designed to reinforce government health services, contraceptives must now be purchased at central government hospitals. According to one camp doctor, legal abortions, which are relatively expensive and provided by hospitals and midwives, are the primary method of family planning among encamped IDPs. Although small enterprise and capacity-building initiatives facilitated by international NGOs typically have gender-inclusive quotas, no projects focus exclusively on the needs of women beyond basic reproductive health education. In addition, no local NGOs are providing services that target displaced women living in camps. Support by local NGOs appears more available to refugees and IDPs living in urban areas, but even there no programs specifically address the needs of victims of GBV. To the extent that Azerbaijan's refugee and IDP women are exposed to sexual or domestic violence, the vast majority manage it under a veil of traditional secrecy.

### Imishli, Beylagan, and Barda

The western region of Azerbaijan bordering Nagorno-Karabakh is home to over a dozen refugee camps clustered around several of Azerbaijan's smaller cities, including Imishli, Beylagan, and Barda. While Baku is modern and cosmopolitan, cities in the west are more expressive of traditional culture. According to one female health provider living and working in an IDP camp on the western frontier, "Tradition says that no one tells family secrets." Health care workers, police, government representatives, and the IDPs themselves echoed this sentiment in interviews.

Nonetheless, both men and women acknowledged various types of violence within their communities, including family conflict, incest, prostitution, and rape. In one anecdote a young woman was required to marry her rapist after she reported the incident to her family. In another, a woman whose jaw was broken by her husband claimed to her doctor that she had fallen down. In yet another, a thirteen-year-old girl was raped and the perpetrator was punished only by being expelled from the community. Some felt that violence—particularly between husbands and wives—was increasing as a result of the tensions associated with years of displacement and economic decline. Divorce rates have reportedly risen. Virtually all those interviewed held that men were the heads of families—several believing that role to be "national law." According to some men and women, a husband's authority could be legitimately expressed in physical acts of discipline and punishment. Conversely, women's disappointed expectations that men should provide for the family's economic well-being have reportedly led to increased conflict instigated by accusing wives.

Although the majority of those interviewed denied the existence of prostitution, several men claimed that the number of prostitutes operating in roadside teahouses and hotels was increasing. They attributed the rise to an increase in single female-headed households. A notable percentage of prostitutes interviewed in research undertaken by an IRC health worker revealed they had been raped before entering the sex trade—and, in fact, had chosen prostitution because the stigma of rape prevented them from resuming a "normal" life.

A camp-based health care provider reiterated concern about prostitution, and assumed that some of those she examined for STIs were engaged in the sex trade, but she had not encountered any patients who indicated or revealed histories of sexual assault. Select health care providers within camps have been briefly trained in the delivery of emergency contraception for rape survivors, but supplies are not on hand and no medical protocols currently exist to respond to victims. Even though standardized protocols exist in the government hospitals—gynecologists are required to conduct forensic exams and report their findings to the police—reported rape cases are extremely rare and then apparently only from unmarried women. One hospital-based gynecologist believed that the few sexual injuries she saw were primarily the result of young girls' sexual precocity and "not understanding the consequences" of sexual intercourse. In any case, unmarried girls who are discovered, through pregnancy or otherwise, to have been sexually active are generally required to marry the man with whom they had sex. (Age of consent and legal marriage for girls is seventeen in Azerbaijan, adjusted downward one year in special cases such as pregnancy.)

According to one police representative, issues of violence against women are settled within the family and do not come to the attention of the authorities. When women do approach police with an incident of domestic abuse—at the rate of one to two cases per month in the Barda area—they are typically advised to attempt to resolve their grievances within their families. In rare instances the police will investigate, but charges are more often dropped by the wives. It is impossible to estimate the number of cases for which there is police and judicial follow-through. Sex-disaggregated data only exist in cases of rape, for which statistics are submitted to the Ministry of Internal Affairs. Nevertheless, the government has reportedly begun to assign a female officer to each police precinct to deal with cases of women and children. It is unclear what the main function of the female officer will be, but such an initiative could improve the reporting rates of women and girl survivors.

## Baku

Although the IDP populations living in makeshift apartment settlements on the outskirts of Baku may be slightly more integrated into their host community than their camp counterparts, they are in some ways just as vulnerable. Housing conditions are often unsanitary, unemployment is widespread, and the cost of living in the capital city is markedly higher than in rural areas. According to one urban IDP group, lack of resources has led to child trafficking—refugee and IDP families knowingly sell their children in order to support the family. In some cases husbands have left Azerbaijan to find employment in Russia, only to disappear, leaving women to support households—a possible determinant to the surge of prostitution in Baku.

The special needs of refugee and IDP girls living in and around Baku have been recognized by international, national, and local organizations. The SCWI, for example, lists refugees and IDPs as its primary

area of concern. Of the local women's NGOs operating in Baku, a few such as Symmetry, the SDWR, and the AWDC have received international financial support and technical assistance to work with women IDPs, providing services ranging from gender and human rights training to charitable relief. As with all services to refugees and IDPs, waning funding has curtailed some activities. Donor-driven competition for resources has also resulted in organizations initiating multiple programs without sufficient staff to administer and implement the varying activities. The NGOs run by IDPs themselves reportedly struggle for resources to remain operational, and are often staffed by volunteers. One such NGO, the Humanitarian Society for Azeri Refugees and Internally Displaced People, has at least five proposals pending, none of which has a promising donor. As in the camps, there do not appear to be any services to address violence against women and girls, even though local NGOs have instituted anti-violence initiatives for the population-at-large. A short-lived local program to provide legal and psychosocial services to refugee and IDP women victims of violence was not refunded, apparently because of organizational problems, and there is no information available about its impact or success. Although a coordinating body was reportedly convened in the mid-1990s to deal with refugee and IDP women's issues, it is no longer operational.

## Summary

Azerbaijan is a country in transition and yet, for the majority of its 800,000 refugees and IDPs, life is not improving. Women and children, as is the case worldwide, are among the most affected. They comprise over 70 percent of the total IDP population in Azerbaijan. In recent years, several research efforts have revealed that violence is one component of the Azeri woman's vulnerability. Notably, none of that research examines violence women may have experienced during or in flight from the Nagorno-Karabakh conflict, though global precedent suggests that some percentage of Azeri women and girls—now refugees and IDPs—were likely victims of conflict-related sexual violence. Tradition apparently compels women to silence; and yet, when directly asked about their experiences of violence, a significant number of Azeri women have acknowledged exposure.

Such disclosure has not yet stimulated services for victims, especially those living as refugees and IDPs. However, various initiatives are underway that may encourage more comprehensive GBV policies and programs, which may in turn positively impact the refugee and IDP populations. The UNDP's GID project and the SCWI have already succeeded in their advocacy for more gender-equitable legislation addressing a variety of women's economic, social, and family rights. The SCWI is currently assisting in revising legislation so that Azerbaijan's laws adhere to European Union standards, and as such spousal abuse will likely be introduced into the criminal code. International donors and organizations, such as the British Embassy, OSI, and OSCE are directly engaged in or are supporting violence prevention programs. IOM has initiated a project to investigate sex trafficking. As mentioned above, local police departments will soon include female officers tasked with responding to concerns of women and children. UNFPA included some messages on violence in its television programming on health. According to a UNIFEM representative, a group of women doctors is interested in improving medical response to domestic violence. Several local women's organizations, such as those listed above, are leading the way in local research and advocacy on women's rights. Symmetry has designed community education regarding violence against women, and the SDWR has developed health services for women working in the sex industry. Their representatives have expressed a strong interest in collaborating more closely with the refugee and IDP populations on GBV issues.

Given the current economic instability in Azerbaijan, none of these efforts or ambitions will be successful without ongoing international financial and technical support. Nor will they have a positive impact on Azerbaijan's refugees and IDPs without a concerted effort to extend programming to these populations, in both urban and rural settings.

## Recommendations

1. The Azerbaijan government and supporting U.N. and other international organizations should undertake nationwide violence prevention and education campaigns that include strategies to target isolated refugee and IDP communities. Campaigns should alert men and women to changing legislation, sensitize men and women to issues related to GBV, and provide information about services available to survivors.

2. The government and supporting U.N. and other international organizations should undertake specific activities to identify, protect, and return women forced into the sex industry. The Ministry of Internal Affairs and the Ministry of Justice should be held accountable for ensuring that cases of trafficking and forced prostitution are thoroughly investigated and that laws against sex traffickers and brothel organizers are exercised to their fullest.

3. The Ministry of Health and relevant international NGOs should ensure that all camp-based medical facilities and government hospitals have standardized protocols for responding to survivors of violence. Hospitals should have rape treatment kits and examination equipment, and services should be confidential and free of cost. Doctors should be trained in appropriate medical response and referral.

4. Government and local NGOs should administer community-based psychosocial programs designed to respond to the needs of women, with particular focus on those exposed to GBV. The government should fund and protect confidential shelters for those women wishing to leave violent situations. Select shelters should be proximate to refugee and IDP centers and settlements, and women should be alerted to their presence. The government should also support local organizations to institute telephone hotlines and other services relevant to potential victims.

5. The Ministry of Internal Affairs, the Ministry of Justice, and the Ministry of Health should require sex disaggregated data on violence against women and girls, and should institute structures for regularly reviewing the data and for adjusting national prevention and response activities.

6. The Ministry of Internal Affairs should ensure that all police officers are trained in the appropriate application of existing laws in the prevention of and response to GBV.

7. The Ministry of Justice should ensure that judges and lawyers are similarly trained regarding

changing laws, and that cases are tried confidentially and expeditiously. The Ministry of Justice
should also support local initiatives that provide
free or reduced-cost legal support to refugees
and IDPs.

8. The SCWI should be fully supported by the
international community and the Azerbaijan government in their efforts to monitor ministries'
implementation of GBV-related policies and
programs.

Notes

1    Symmetry, *Women and Violence* (Baku, 1999), 27.

2    U.S. Department of State, *Country Reports on Human Rights Practices:
     Azerbaijan* (Washington, D.C., 2001), 1.

3    U.S. Department of State, *Country Reports on Human Rights Practices:
     Azerbaijan*, 1.

4    United Nations Development Program (UNDP), *Azerbaijan Human
     Development Report, 2000* (Baku, 2000), 55-57.

5    UNDP, *The Report on the Status of Women of Azerbaijan Republic* (Baku, 2000), 53.

6    UNDP, *Azerbaijan Human Development Report 2000*, 22; see also, UNDP, *The
     Report on the Status of Women of Azerbaijan*, 17.

7    U.S. Department of State, *Country Reports on Human Rights Practices:
     Azerbaijan*, 14.

8    U.S. Department of State, *Country Reports on Human Rights Practices:
     Azerbaijan*, 14.

9    UNDP, *The Report on the Status of Women of Azerbaijan*, 21.

10   UNDP, *The Report on the Status of Women of Azerbaijan*, 23.

11   UNDP, *The Report on the Status of Women of Azerbaijan*, 10.

12   UNDP, *The Report on the Status of Women of Azerbaijan*, 12.

13   Symmetry, *Women and Violence*, 30.

14   Azerbaijan Women and Development Center, *The Problem of Exploitation of
     Women in Family: The Ways of Its Solution* (Baku, 1999), 9.

15   J. Kerimova, S. F. Posner, Y. T. Brown, J. Schmidt, S. Hillis, S. Meikle, J.
     Lewis, and A. Duerr, "Factors Associated with Self-Reported Forced Sex
     Among Azerbaijani Women" (unpublished abstract presented at the
     Reproductive Health for Refugees Conference, Washington, D.C.,
     December 2000).

16   Pathfinder International, *Knowledge, Attitude and Practice of Refugees and IDPs
     Towards Reproductive Health and Family Planning Issues* (Baku, 2000), 30.

17   U.S. Department of State, *Country Reports on Human Rights Practices:
     Azerbaijan*, 14.

18   Pathfinder, *Knowledge, Attitude and Practice* (Baku, 2000), 15.

19   U.S. Department of State, *Country Reports on Human Rights Practices:
     Azerbaijan*, 14.

20   International Rescue Committee, "Report on Prostitution in Roadside
     Teahouses and Cafes" (unpublished report of the Health Education
     Program, Azerbaijan, 1999), 1.

21   UNDP, *Azerbaijan Human Development Report 2000*, 45.

22   U.S. Department of State, *Country Reports on Human Rights Practices:
     Azerbaijan*, 17.

23   International Organization for Migration (untitled internal report, Baku,
     June 2000), 23.

# Post-conflict Situation in
# *Bosnia and Herzegovina*

June 18-27, 2001

## Background

### Historical Context

In March 1992, following the lead of Slovenia and Croatia, Bosnia and Herzegovina (BiH) declared autonomy from the crumbling Socialist Federal Republic of Yugoslavia. Under Marshal Tito's extended post-World War II rule, each of Yugoslavia's six republics retained the constitutional right to secede. But when BiH moved to exercise this right twelve years after Tito's death, its independence referendum was met—by Yugoslavia's increasingly extremist Serbian nationalist movement—with the same outrage and resentment that had instigated earlier military offensives in Slovenia and Croatia. Whereas Slovenia's war lasted ten days and Croatia's seven months, the conflict in BiH persisted over three years, killing and "disappearing" an estimated quarter million of the 4.1 million population, displacing another two million, and devastating virtually every sector of BiH's society. In some measure, the protracted war was the catastrophic outcome of what was once perceived as a strength of BiH: its multiculturalism.

Before 1992, some 42 percent of Bosnians were Muslim, 33 percent Serb, and 18 percent Croat; the small percentage remaining was comprised of Roma and other minority populations. At the outset of BiH's war, Croat and Muslim factions united in opposition to the nationalist Bosnian Serbs, but rising tensions and territorial disputes led to a Bosnian Croat separatist movement that ignited a "war within a war" and fueled fighting throughout the country. The

nationalistic strategies that defined the ensuing conflict aspired to ethnic homogeneity. As such, ethnic cleansing—expelling undesirables from targeted towns and regions through such tactics as murder, rape, terror, and propaganda—became a hallmark of the war. Two years into BiH's depredation, international mediation succeeded in reunifying Muslim and Croat forces, whose subsequent combined military success forced the Serbs into negotiations. In December 1995, the historic Dayton Peace Accords were signed, establishing under the "state" of BiH two separate "entities," each with political, legislative, and judicial autonomy. One, the Federation of Bosnia and Herzegovina (hereafter "the Federation") comprises 51 percent of BiH territory and is home to Bosniacs (Muslims), Croats, and several ethnic minority groups. The other, the Republika Srpska (RS), covers the remaining 49 percent, and is home to the majority of Bosnian Serbs.

### Current Government

Since the implementation of the Dayton Accords, BiH's simultaneous peace process and transition to a pluralist democracy have been overseen by multiple international intergovernmental organizations. The Office of the High Representative (OHR) is responsible for the overall civilian implementation of the Dayton Accords. The United Nations Mission in Bosnia and Herzegovina (UNMIBH) is responsible for maintaining peace and is primarily comprised of the Judicial System Assessment Program (JSAP) and the civilian International Police Task Force (IPTF). The Organization for Security and Cooperation in

Europe (OSCE) deals with democratization; the United Nations High Commissioner for Refugees (UNHCR) addresses the rights and return of refugees and the internally displaced; and the United Nations Office of the High Commissioner for Human Rights (OHCHR) monitors and assists in the implementation of trainings and reforms that facilitate social and economic rights. U.N. development agencies are in charge of the long-term socioeconomic, cultural, and political development of BiH society. Military field operations in Bosnia are overseen by the NATO's Stabilization Force of the Partnership for Peace (SFOR).

However intricate, the organizational complexity of international oversight and protection in BiH pales in comparison to BiH's own institutional structures, where the independent and unique Federation and RS governments present ongoing challenges to the goal of national unity. The national- or "state"-level government of BiH has a parliamentary legislature with representatives from both the Federation and RS; a constitutional court; and an executive Council of Ministers (CoM). The CoM is composed of six departments responsible for areas of national jurisdiction, including foreign affairs, civil affairs, communications, foreign trade and economic affairs, European integration, human rights and refugees, and state treasury. Practically speaking, however, the six ministries rely on the Federation and RS entities to enforce its rulings, and control over the social, economic, health, security, and judicial sectors—virtually all aspects of public administration—is the preserve of the respective entity governments.[1]

## Status of Women

Inside this labyrinth, and in the wake of a resurgent patriarchy that accompanied the rise in nationalism preceding and during the war,[2] women have suffered from a lack of government-level representation and support. Despite the fact that the Convention on the Elimination of All Forms of Discrimination Against Women (CEDAW) was ratified first by Yugoslavia, later by the newly independent BiH, and acceded to again through the Dayton Accords, the Accords contain no separate provisions of their own about gender.[3] As a consequence, according to a 2000 U.N. Common Country Study, gender equity was neglected in the early years of reconstruction: "Most policy and program activities have been implemented by and for men" such that "the position of women in BiH

has deteriorated markedly since the early 1990s, with their problems still seen as marginal."[4] This failure to recognize officially the needs of women flies in the face of the special impact the war has had on them. Aside from their well-documented exposure to GBV described below, it is widely believed—though undocumented—that high numbers of women were widowed by war, contributing to a post-conflict sex ratio imbalance in which females average 55 percent of the population.[5] A 1998 World Bank study estimated that women headed 16 to 20 percent of all households.[6] Even so, property and inheritance rights still favor men; domicile reconstruction efforts have no special provisions for women; and the limited reproductive health services available to women are underutilized because of cultural norms and prohibitive fees. Employment is especially problematic for displaced, rural, middle-aged, and older women whose levels of education and professional expertise are significantly lower than their male counterparts.[7] Even in cases where women find work, their wages may be as much as 20 to 50 percent lower than those of men in comparable positions.[8]

Because of these gender inequities, some international government-based initiatives have been introduced in the last several years to advance the rights of women. OSCE has been crucial to the success of quotas improving women's representation in politics—with women officials jumping in 1998 from 5 percent and below to 15 percent and above in select state and entity bodies. OHCHR, whose head of office has been a staunch and well-respected advocate for local women, has lobbied for improved legislation and was the primary force behind the early success of OHR's Gender Coordination Group. The international community in BiH established this group in 1999 as the first inter-agency initiative to address gender issues. Elizabeth Rehn, the Special Representative of the Secretary General to UNMIBH from 1997 to 1999, was outspoken in her criticism of UNMIBH's failure to incorporate women in its ranks and in the ranks of the local police force. She also publicly acknowledged the phenomenon of domestic violence, serving as an inspiration to many Bosnian women and women's organizations.[9] More recently, the United Nations Development Program (UNDP) has taken on the task of assisting each entity government to produce a CEDAW report, and the Independent Bureau of Humanitarian Issues (IBHI), funded by the Finnish government, is supporting gender mainstreaming in government and civil society institutions throughout BiH. The IBHI is also spearheading a project to facilitate the Federation government's newly established Gender Center (planned for replication in RS), which currently suffers from vaguely formulated mandates.[10]

Although U.N. and other government oversight institutions have made recent advances in addressing gender issues, the most powerful voice for women has come from the growing civil sector—local women's organizations and the international organizations that support them. It was women's NGOs, in fact, that launched BiH's civil society during the years of conflict, introducing welfare programs for refugees, elderly, and other vulnerable groups, as well as counseling and medical care for survivors of war-related rape.[11] In 1996 these NGOs converged at the first Conference of Women in BiH to strategize about their post-conflict roles. Many NGOs born during the war continue, and others have started subsequent to the Dayton Accords—a mushrooming felt by some to reflect women's "exclusion from representative and executive-level politics."[12] It is this sector that has had particular influence in advancing programming often peripheral to government agendas, such as prevention and response activities related to GBV.

## Gender-based Violence

### During Conflict

International coverage of sexual violence during the first year of the Bosnian conflict—however sensational and compromising to survivor confidentiality—set the stage for modern reporting on the issue, stimulating public interest in GBV as a component of warfare and heightening sensitivity to the phenomenon in subsequent conflicts, most notably Rwanda and Kosovo. By now much has been published about the systematic and strategic rape of women and girls during the war in BiH, though precise data remain elusive. In September 1992 the BiH government released a report citing evidence of the rape by Serbs of at least 13,000 women and girls, the majority of whom were Muslim, hypothesizing that the actual number was closer to 50,000.[13] A follow-up study by a European commission suggested that the numbers were around 20,000.[14] Weighing in around the same time, the Commission for War Crimes in the former Yugoslavia alleged that 800 Serb women were victims

of rape by Muslim forces.[15] Regardless of numbers and whoever the perpetrators, it is widely agreed that rape was a systematic rather than incidental part of the war. Women and girls were sexually assaulted in the presence of family members, sequestered in rape camps, forced into sexual servitude, intentionally impregnated, and subject to genital mutilation. There are also accounts of sexual abuses suffered by men and boys, including injuries to sex organs, castration, rape, and forced sex among imprisoned male relatives.[16]

Although few men have been willing to come forward with testimonies of torture and GBV suffered during the war, women's experiences have been somewhat easier to get access to. Some have even been collected in the book *I Begged Them to Kill Me*, published by an association of concentration camp survivors.[17] Although the exposure of women victims of rape in the international media further stigmatized some of those who came forward,[18] their willingness to report had a historic effect on international law as it relates to GBV. In a landmark verdict by the International Criminal Tribunal for the former Yugoslavia (ICTY), sentences handed down in 2001 to three Serbs were the first ever based solely on crimes of sexual violence against women, as well as the first to recognize GBV as a crime against humanity. Survivors' reports also stimulated funding for psychosocial programming, which has in turn raised awareness about other forms of violence experienced by women.

### Beyond Conflict

One of the most pressing forms of GBV identified by local women's NGOs is domestic violence. Violence in the BiH home is apparently not only normative, but an expression of the widely accepted right of husbands to discipline their wives. According to a local opinion poll conducted by the Sarajevo-based women's NGO Zena Zenama, 44 percent of the 169 male and female respondents felt that violence against women in BiH was "extremely high," due primarily to the "deep roots" of patriarchal traditions.[19] Of one hundred women polled by another NGO, Zena Sa Une in Bihac, 96 percent concurred that women should be punished if they do something wrong in the marriage or in the home.[20] Given these attitudes, it is perhaps not surprising that no legal provisions specifically addressing domestic violence or rape in marriage existed in Yugoslavia's legal code; nor were there any services for survivors before the war.

After the war, several women's NGO captured, through service statistics and surveys, the nature and scope of domestic violence in BiH. Of over five hundred women from the Zenica region interviewed in 1998 by Medica Zenica, 23 percent had been beaten by their partner, and, of those, a quarter had been beaten multiple times.[21] A subsequent study using the same survey instrument to analyze GBV within Zenica's minority Roma population reported that 44 percent of 106 women interviewed were survivors of partner violence, 33 percent of whom had experienced violence over an extended period.[22] In research conducted by a Mostar NGO, Zena BiH, one-third of one thousand women randomly interviewed in the Mostar area had personally experienced domestic violence.[23] The NGO United Women, based in Banja Luka, recorded in its service statistics that of the seven hundred women utilizing their legal counsel over three years, 70 percent reported domestic violence.[24] Similar service statistics from hotlines in Gorazde, Sarajevo, and Mostar recorded reports of domestic violence, exposing the issue of not only partner violence but also violence against mothers by their sons.[25]

As is often the case in post-conflict settings where no data preexist, it is difficult to determine whether domestic violence in BiH increased following the war or whether reporting has increased with the introduction of victim services. A rise in trafficking of women, on the other hand, has been directly attributed to the post-war environment, where the presence of an international community, high levels of corruption, and a fragile transitional economy conspire to promote the sex trade. The success of sex trafficking in BiH may also be related to the historic indifference toward "voluntary" local prostitution, which also increased following the war.[26] Although prostitution is illegal, it is considered a private affair and is rarely prosecuted. Public complacency about prostitution is evident in the outcome of research undertaken by a women's NGO in RS; when surveyors queried people on the streets about the existence of brothels and their illegality, the vast majority of respondents knew of their existence and believed their activities to be legal.[27]

A 2000 report of the Joint Trafficking Project of UNMIBH and the OHCHR describes BiH as a major destination point for women trafficked from Eastern Europe. The report attributes the success of the sex trade to "obstruction, obfuscation, and simple passivity" that "permeate the law enforcement and policy apparatus of the State at every level."[28] Charges aired by an IPTF police officer in 2000 implicated U.N. and SFOR personnel in the promotion of the sex trade, to which UNMIBH issued denials, declaring that those found guilty would receive punishment "commensurate with the gravity of the offences."[29] Following a series of raids on brothels in Prijedor, six officers were in fact discharged for using the services of the women they were rescuing, though no declamatory marks were recorded in their military records.[30] Despite the possible complicity of officials, over three hundred trafficked women and girls ranging from thirteen to thirty-six years of age have been rescued since 1999. After receiving temporary shelter by the International Organization for Migration (IOM), they are returned to their countries of origin, primarily Moldova and Romania.[31] Testimonies of their experience to UNMIBH and IOM suggest that trafficked women are held in brothels against their will, sometimes tortured, often forced to have unprotected sex, and denied access to health services by brothel owners.

## Current GBV-related Programming

Although the Dayton Accords did not recognize gender—or GBV—within its articles, psychosocial programs targeting women proliferated during and after the war. Many of these short-lived programs provided only curative services to rape and torture survivors and were based on a generalized trauma treatment model. They did not facilitate ongoing programming to address GBV as a pervasive social phenomenon. Even in the case of the UNHCR-administered Bosnian Women's Initiative (BWI)— whose initial $5 million donation from the U.S. Department of State in 1996 was the largest source of post-war funds for Bosnian women's empowerment activities—grants supporting GBV programming were generally small-scale and short term, and funding distribution lacked an overall strategy for GBV prevention and response.[32] As a result, by 1998, when OXFAM conducted research throughout the Balkans on domestic violence, its findings indicated that in BiH no standardized services existed *at any level* for survivors. Police, health services, government-run centers for social work, and most legal advocates were ill-prepared to respond to the issue of GBV. Furthermore, legislation was not supportive of victims, requiring women seeking prosecution for anything other than "grievous bodily injury" to initiate the legal process at their own expense.[33]

In spite of the early limitations of post-war GBV prevention and response programming, several initiatives instituted collaboratively by local women and international organizations during and directly following the war set the stage for later activities. These initiatives not only improved local awareness and response to violence, some provided models for programming that were replicated elsewhere in BiH. They also formed a critical advocacy base for GBV issues, encouraging the eventual involvement of many of BiH's major international institutions in GBV prevention and response activities, and influencing the design of more gender-equitable legislation. Those considered in the vanguard include Medica Zenica in Zenica, Anima in Gorazde, Koraci Nade in Mostar, and United Women in Banja Luka.

## Zenica

Of the psychosocial projects developed to address war-related violence against women, Medica Zenica was the first. It is also the most comprehensive and well-known anti-violence NGO operating in BiH. Conceived in 1993 by a German activist working in collaboration with local women professionals, Medica quickly expanded its original mandate of responding to the needs of raped women to include multiple support services for women in need. With ongoing training and financial support by a German philanthropic organization, which evolved as a result of the work of Medica's founders, Medica has grown from a fifteen-member to an eighty-member association. It consists of autonomous yet interrelated projects, including a counseling center, medical services, a hotline, and two safe houses with education, training, and micro-enterprise activities. Its research and communications unit, Infoteka, serves as a global model for advocacy activities that are critical to the prevention of and response to GBV. Infoteka was the first to conduct population-based research on violence against women in BiH, and the only local NGO to have research published. With international training on social marketing from agencies such as CARE, Infoteka has also designed multiple community education campaigns for which they have had measurable success.

Medica also inspired the creation of one of the first free legal centers in post-war BiH, the Center of Legal Assistance for Women (CLAW). With support from the international NGO Kvinna till Kvinna, the Center has been operating in Zenica since 1996. In addition to providing direct services to women on issues such as property rights, CLAW actively supported the creation of a network of legal centers operating across BiH, whose activities have been critical to formulating more gender-sensitive legislation.[34] In collaboration with a lead organization, the Sarajevo-based International Human Rights Law Group (IHRLG), CLAW and other legal advocates contributed to a comprehensive analysis of laws related to women's human rights in BiH. The resulting reference publication not only identifies existing laws relevant to areas such as labor, health, GBV, education, and political participation but also provides recommendations that have formed the basis of efforts to draft more gender-equitable laws.[35]

In recognition of Medica's expertise, the OHCHR chose Zenica as the location for a 1999 pilot project designed to support the prevention and prosecution of GBV by creating a coordinated community network of services for women survivors of violence. Several international institutions and organizations, such as UNMIBH, OXFAM, and IHRLG worked with OHCHR and Medica to establish protocols for case management within sectors involving the police, social and health services, and judiciary, and to reinforce sectoral links. Specific project activities included sector-based trainings, the implementation of a multi-sectoral task force, and a community-based GBV awareness campaign.

Representatives from Medica have hailed the pilot project as a success. Whereas before cooperation with NGOs, police, and judiciary was problematic, the trainings have facilitated coordination and mutual support among the sectors, resulting in more effective and efficient services for women in the Zenica region. However, lack of funds has precluded replication of activities in other parts of BiH.

## Gorazde

The International Rescue Committee (IRC) was the first international NGO to assess the post-war sexual and reproductive health of women living in Gorazde, a decimated border city surrounded on three sides by RS territory. Several GBV-related questions within IRC's 1997 survey revealed high levels of domestic violence: 55 percent of women interviewed knew at least one woman who had been beaten by a husband or boyfriend.[36] IRC responded to the findings by supporting the local NGO Anima's effort to establish BiH's first GBV hotline. As part of a campaign to promote the hotline, a local well-known media figure hosted regular radio programs in which she acknowledged her personal exposure to domestic abuse. Anima also conducted outreach to local police and social services, facilitating sectoral coordination and case management of women reporting to the hotline. The Gorazde police began disaggregating statistics on domestic violence, an action unprecedented throughout BiH. Their data suggest that police intervention combined with community education has been a success in Gorazde. According to local police representatives, an initial surge in police reporting subsequent to the media campaign was followed by a decrease in both new and repeat cases of domestic violence. In a similarly unprecedented move, the center for social work in Gorazde assigned a worker to deal exclusively with domestic violence cases. IRC's 1999 follow-up survey found that respondents who knew a domestic violence victim had dropped from 55 percent to 36 percent, and those agreeing that a man is entitled to hit his wife "if she does something wrong" dropped from 29 percent to 14 percent.

Anima's hotline was a model for subsequent hotlines now in place in Bihac, Mostar, Zenica, Tuzla, Travnik, and Sarajevo. The Tuzla, Zenica, and Sarajevo lines not only provide phone counseling but also offer follow-up services such as referrals to shelters and counseling. Most recently, the Federation government has instituted a federal system of hotlines, with a plan to add more. It also plans to coordinate with the RS, whose only hotline currently runs out of Banja Luka. Despite the success of the hotlines, just one offers 24-hour support, and the majority must generate private funding. The Gorazde hotline, for example, was shut down after two years for lack of funds, even though in IRC's 1999 follow-up survey 95 percent thought the hotline was a good idea, and 89 percent said they would use the hotline if they were in an abusive relationship.[37] Attempts to solicit potential donors continue to be unsuccessful, and the Gorazde hotline remains shut down.

## Mostar

The divided town of Mostar is a catastrophic example of Bosnia's "war within a war." At the outset of

fighting, Mostar's Croats and Bosniacs united to rout the Serbs, but later turned against one another in a conflict that split the town along ethnic lines, with the Croats living in the east and the Bosniacs in the west. In the midst of war, Marie Stopes International initiated emergency services targeting displaced, refugee, and war-traumatized women on both sides of Mostar's divide. Although the activities in Mostar are similar to others spearheaded by Stope Nade throughout BiH and Croatia, the sustained breadth and reach of the Mostar-based programs are exemplary, especially in light of Mostar's continuing ethnic tensions.

A primary initial objective of the Stope Nade program was to identify and assist women victims of war-related rape through the grassroots provision of psychosocial and health services. Their approach departed from BiH's plethora of psychosocial programs in that Stope Nade relied heavily on local women to design and provide services, which in turn enhanced program flexibility and cultural sensitivity. Early difficulty gaining access to rape victims necessitated a shift to a broader mandate, inclusive of all war-affected women. A team of local women established therapeutic "talking groups" in women's centers, private homes, and vacant buildings throughout Mostar, as well as educational and occupational activity groups. Within two years of its inception, the Stope Nade program was fully incorporated as a local NGO, receiving ongoing funding from Marie Stopes International, Kvinna till Kvinna, and other donors. Now known as Koraci Nade, the organization runs four centers in east and west Mostar and one center in nearby RS. Operations in east and west Mostar as well as the RS—unusual among NGOs in the region which do not typically work across ethnic boundaries—allow for activities that bridge ethnic difference. In fact, the center in RS was the first in postwar BiH where Croats, Bosniacs, and Serbs convened. Each center provides psychosocial, educational, occupational, and health services targeting women and youth, and each promotes a self-help model. Koraci Nade also conducts mobile outreach to women in need of legal and counseling services and media campaigns on issues such as adolescent development and domestic violence.

Although the Koraci Nade program does not exclusively target women survivors of GBV, it has basic forensic and counseling protocols in place. Other organizations have since developed in Mostar with similarly broad-based activities. For example, the women's NGOs Sumeja and Ideja both provide a mix of legal, psychosocial, and educational services to women in Mostar and surrounding towns. The only Mostar organization notable for specifically targeting survivors is Zena BiH—its hotline and research initiatives directly serve victims of violence. Although Zena BiH sees a strong need for a shelter, lack of funding has prevented the NGO from being able to provide anything other than temporary accommodations to women on an informal, ad hoc basis.

Insofar as Zena BiH is the only Mostar NGO specifically addressing the needs of survivors, the result is that GBV-related coordination and cooperation among women's NGOs and other sectors, especially the police and judiciary, have not been developed in Mostar. In contrast to Zena BiH's research finding that Mostar women experience high levels of violence, a senior representative of the Mostar police maintains that there are no reported cases of prostitution or trafficking, and that the incidence of other forms of GBV is low—though exact numbers are impossible to obtain because the police do not disaggregate data on reported cases. Pending funding, the pilot project to create a coordinated community network of GBV services initiated by OHCHR in Zenica is planned for replication in Mostar.

## Banja Luka

The largest city in RS and the site of extensive ethnic cleansing during the war, Banja Luka is one of a limited number of places in RS with activities targeting GBV. One leading women's organization is United Women (UW), a local NGO established in 1996 to provide support to war-affected women. Their service statistics represent the only data available on domestic violence in RS. Over a four-year period 70 percent of UW's clients came forward with complaints of partner violence. Staffed with a paralegal, lawyer, social worker, psychologist, and assisted by a cadre of volunteer professionals, UW operates the RS's single hotline. The organization also provides case management and psychosocial services to women in need and manages a legal program that includes free counsel and court representation.

A UW collaboration with a local human rights organization, the Helsinki Citizens Assembly (hCa), has resulted in the groundbreaking project "Woman Today." The project's community roundtable series on issues relevant to women set a standard for community education that has since been imitated by local and international NGOs throughout RS. When first introduced in 1997, the project limited its topics to women's health and other "neutral" concerns. After gaining a reputable footing, roundtable discussions among an average of twenty to forty community participants embraced more controversial subjects such as human rights, domestic violence, and equality. Several of the roundtables were broadcast over radio and television, with their contents recorded in reports subsequently distributed to local and international organizations and government institutions.

Since collaborating on the "Woman Today" roundtables, hCa has developed modules for elementary school education on issues of gender, tolerance, conflict resolution, and domestic violence. The large base of hCa membership has made the implementation of the modules elsewhere in RS easier. The organization's board also supports UW's legal offices, and hCa members volunteer on the UW hotline. The cooperation exemplified in UW's and hCa's activities provides a paradigm for extending NGO impact. Roundtable discussions and trainings have increased awareness and sensitivity of local police and judiciary, as well as coordination among the sectors. The service statistics from UW were also used in advocacy to create laws in the RS specifically addressing domestic violence.

## Sarajevo

It is often the case that GBV activities radiate from progressive initiatives established in a given country's capital city. In BiH the opposite may be true. Field-based NGOs such as Medica Zenica, Anima, Koraci Nade, Zena BiH, and UW have given voice to women's concerns throughout BiH, highlighting GBV as an issue of national importance. The reach of most of these NGOs—in terms of both service delivery and advocacy—has been significantly enhanced by the sustained financial and technical support of the international community, most notably from donors with overt mandates to support women's rights, such as Medica Mondiale, Delphi International/STAR Network, OXFAM, and Kvinna till Kvinna. More recently, and perhaps as a result of the impact of field-based programming, GBV-related projects have accelerated in the capital of Sarajevo. A domestic violence shelter supported by an Italian NGO opened in

2000, and is operating at its maximum fifteen-to twenty-client capacity. Zena Zenama, a multiethnic and multiservice local women's rights NGO, also introduced GBV activities in 2000, conducting the only community-based research on violence against Sarajevo women and establishing hotline services several hours each day. Another Sarajevo hotline offering 24-hour support, Tele Apel Telefon, subsequently opened with funding from the Netherlands NGO Healthnet International and is now leading the newly established network of hotlines in the Federation.

Among Sarajevo's international institutions actively addressing GBV issues, the OHCHR has taken the lead in raising awareness within national and international bodies, as well as in facilitating coordination and linkages among women's organizations, both governmental and non-governmental, international and local. Collaborative efforts of the OHCHR, OHR, IHRLG, and local NGOs have resulted in changes in legislation in the RS and the Federation. Each entity now has provisions addressing domestic violence—though their differing degrees of protection are still subject to revision. UNMIBH has implemented sensitization training for its IPTF officers on how to respond to domestic violence and, most recently, has launched a nationwide media campaign encouraging survivors to seek police protection and support.

In 1999 OHCHR began a joint effort with UNMIBH to address the issue of trafficking of women, stimulating several local, governmental, and international initiatives. Draft legislation criminalizing trafficking is currently pending entity approval. The IHRLG has produced a trafficking training manual for legal professionals, and select NGOs have been organized by the OHCHR into a consultative anti-trafficking coalition. OHR's inter-agency Gender Coordination Group now facilitates a subgroup on trafficking, and the BiH government has formed an interministerial task force that has produced a national platform of action. The IOM, which conducted a community sensitization campaign on trafficking throughout BiH, currently manages a shelter for trafficking survivors in Sarajevo and oversees survivor repatriation. The United Nations Population Fund (UNFPA) is developing a proposal to augment health services for rescued trafficking victims. UNMIBH recently launched a Special Trafficking Operational Program (STOP) to improve and hasten police investigations

regarding trafficking, one component of which is to introduce more women officers into the IPTF field offices. Select local police precincts have also established specialized trafficking units, increasing demand for female police recruits. At the regional level, a task force sponsored by the Stability Pact for Southeastern Europe (SEE) was launched in 2000. Its priority areas of prevention, protection, return, and reintegration are coordinated by participating SEE governments, international institutions such as OSCE, the Council of Europe, IOM, OHCHR, the United Nations Children's Fund (UNICEF), and other international and local NGOs.

## Summary

During and following the war in BiH, programs focusing on the needs of women survivors of war-related sexual assault received considerable humanitarian support. The strong leadership of local women and the long-term, substantive, and flexible financial and technical support of donor organizations sustains those programs that remain in operation. Such support has allowed local organizations to adapt to the shifting needs of their constituencies, and to create imaginative and culturally appropriate GBV initiatives. Such support has also been the exception. In spite of research and service statistics suggesting GBV is a pervasive post-war phenomenon, the majority of communities throughout BiH still have very limited GBV prevention and response activities. Competition for funding, as well as limited donor support of GBV-related activities, has compelled many women's organizations to diversify their range of activities, such that GBV activities are infrequently afforded primary focus. Where targeted GBV activities have been supported—in Zenica and Gorazde, for example—outcomes have included increased community awareness and survivor reporting. These outcomes are the result of institutionalized coordination among local NGOs, police, social services, and the judiciary.

Although international and national government structures have generally lagged behind NGOs in promoting attention to GBV, the activities of local and international NGOs, combined with the efforts of the OHCHR and the work of the members of OHR's Gender Coordination Group, have in the last several years stimulated entity and state action. These include adoption of new legislation addressing domestic violence, creation of a national plan of action to address trafficking, and the Federation's network of hotlines. Despite these advances, international and local advocacy has yet to result in government-supported protocols or programs addressing GBV. Medical documentation is usually a prerequisite to prosecuting rape and domestic violence cases, but survivors must pay for services. Health establishments are not supported or monitored for quality of GBV-related services, nor are they required to submit GBV data at the local, entity, or state level. Local police have had limited training on GBV and are similarly not required to collect or submit GBV-related data. Accounts from women's NGOs suggest that the majority of local police remain reluctant, as in the case of Mostar's police representative, to intervene in domestic disputes. Many members of the judiciary are reportedly not sensitized to new laws, especially in higher courts, and there have been no efforts to analyze judicial response to GBV cases. Most centers for social work, which exist throughout BiH and could be a natural entry point for survivors seeking support services, have received no training in GBV and are not required to collect and submit data related to GBV.

## Recommendations

1. Legislation and policies regarding GBV must be brought into accordance by the state at entity levels, in line with standards set forth by the European Union (EU). Mechanisms for sustainability of GBV prevention and response activities must also be established and monitored by the state. All ministries and organizations should be apprised of the basic standards required for alignment with EU regulations.

2. Ministries responsible for the reform and oversight of health care must establish systems to improve medical response to GBV by supporting the training of health care providers and collecting and monitoring GBV-related health statistics. Forensic evaluations should be standardized and should be free of cost to survivors.

3. Ministries of justice should undertake research on the judiciary's awareness and application of new laws relevant to GBV. They should work with international and local experts such as IHRLG and CLAW in order to train judges and lawyers on local laws and international conventions such

as CEDAW. The numerous legal aid programs that international NGOs currently run to assist refugee and internally displaced women with property claims should incorporate GBV into their service provision.

4. Ministries responsible for internal security should require all police cadets to receive training in prevention of and response to GBV. Females should be actively recruited to the police forces, and in addition to trafficking, each police precinct should operate units specializing in domestic violence and sexual assault. Sex disaggregated data on GBV-related cases should be collected and monitored at the local, municipal, entity, and state levels, and community policing initiatives should be developed accordingly. The IPTF should review and improve its implementation of trainings on GBV, further extending them to SFOR.

5. Ministries responsible for social welfare should require in their policy guidelines that centers for social work provide supportive case management to survivors and that they support this policy through comprehensive and standardized trainings. Training curricula should rely on the expertise of centers for social work such as the one in Gorazde as well as that of local women's NGOs with experience providing GBV services. All centers should be required to collect and submit data on GBV cases, to be regularly monitored by relevant ministries in order to improve social services. Telephone hotlines should similarly be encouraged to collect and submit standardized data. Wherever possible, hotlines should operate on a 24-hour basis. The Federation's network of hotlines should be replicated in RS.

6. Community coordination projects such as the one spearheaded by the OHCHR in Zenica should be evaluated and replicated throughout BiH in the hope of establishing multisectoral community task forces to address GBV that include representatives of health, police, centers for social work, local NGOs, and beneficiaries.

7. The entity-level Gender Center, currently in operation in the Federation and planned for replication in RS, should incorporate in its evolving functions the oversight of ministries' implementation of GBV-related policies and protocols.

8. Given the damaged economy and the current fragmentation of the BiH government, international donors should continue to support local NGOs in the provision of GBV-related prevention, response, and research activities, following the long-term financial and technical support model that has been critical to the success of existing projects. Recognizing programs' ongoing need for international funding, self-sustainability should not be a condition of donor support.

9. International institutions and organizations, especially those participating in the Gender Coordination Group, should redouble efforts to improve collaboration among local NGOs, as well as between local NGOs and other sectors. If the U.N. agencies are held accountable to their mandates, they should not only support GBV programs as a priority for protecting women, but they should also pressure the BiH government to do the same.

10. GBV programs should research and introduce appropriate interventions for male survivors that embrace the special concerns of men and boys. Projects currently targeting men—such as the demobilization and reintegration initiatives—should include GBV prevention and response in their education and direct services, as well as psychological and alcohol abuse counseling.

## Notes

1   United Nations Office of the Resident Coordinator for Development Operations, *Common Country Study: The Transiton to Development—Challenges and Priorities for UN Development Assistance to Bosnia-Herzegovina* (Sarajevo, 2000), 20.

2   A. Lithander, *Engendering the Peace Process: A Gender Approach to Dayton and Beyond* (Stockholm, 2000), 18.

3   Lithander, *Engendering the Peace Process*, 3.

4   U.N. Office of the Resident Coordinator, *Common Country Study*, 10.

5   Memorandum, United Nations High Commissioner for Refugees (UNHCR), "Situation of Women in BiH—From UNHCR's Perspective" (Sarajevo, April 2000), Annex 1.

6   World Bank, *Bosnia and Herzegovina: The Priority Reconstruction Program; Achievements and 1998 Needs* (Sarajevo, 1998), 49.

7   UNHCR, "Situation of Women in BiH," 3-5.

8   M. Walsh, *Aftermath: The Impact of Conflict on Women in Bosnia and Herzegovina*, U.S. Agency for International Development Center for Development Information and Evaluation, Working Paper No. 302, (Washington, D.C., 2000), 5.

9   Lithander, *Engendering the Peace Process*, 35-37.

10  U.N., *Common Country Study*, 27.

11  Walsh, *Aftermath*, 2.

12  Walsh, *Aftermath*, 2.

13  V. Nikolic-Ristanovic, "Living Without Democracy and Peace: Violence Against Women in the Former Yugoslavia," *Violence Against Women* 5, no. 1 (January 1999): 67.

14  M. Olujic, "Embodiment of Terror: Gendered Violence Peacetime and Wartime in Croatia and Bosnia-Herzegovina," *Medical Anthropology Quarterly* 12, no. 1 (1998): 40.

15  Nikolic-Ristanovic, "Living Without Democracy and Peace," 67.

16  Olujic, "Embodiment of Terror," 41.

17  Cited in Z. Mudrovic, *Sexual and Gender-based Violence in Post-Conflict Regions: The Bosnia and Herzegovina Case* (paper presented at UNFPA Conference on Women in Conflict, Bratislava, November 13, 2001).

18  Nikolic-Ristanovic, "Living Without Democracy and Peace," 68.

19  Zena Zenama (unpublished, untitled internal report on research findings, Sarajevo, 2000).

20  Cited in C. Clark, "SGBV Research Initiatives from the field: Lessons Learned" (draft paper to be presented at the Global Health Conference, Washington, D.C., 2002), 9.

21  Medica Zenica, *To Live Without Violence* (Zenica, 1998), 53.

22  Medica Zenica, *How We Live* (Zenica, 2001), 27.

23  Mostar, "Women of BiH, 2001: Analysis of the Survey on Violence," cited in Mudrovic, *The Bosnia and Herzegovina Case*, 8.

24  Clark, "SGBV Research," 11.

25  Walsh, *Aftermath*, 9.

26  UNHCR, "Situation of Women in BiH," 7.

27  Clark, "SGBV Research," 1.

28  Joint Trafficking Project of the UN Mission in Bosnia-Herzegovina (UNMIBH) and the Office of the High Commissioner for Human Rights (OHCHR), *Trafficking in Human Beings in Bosnia and Herzegovina: A Summary Report* (Sarajevo, 2000), 2.

29  T. Domi, *BCR* 264 (July 2001): 1.

30  T. Domi, *BCR* 264 (July 2001): 1.

31  Personal correspondence from staff member of UNMIBH, Office of the High Commissioner for Human Rights Internal Statistics, Sarajevo, June 2001.

32  UNHCR, *Women Transforming Themselves and Society: Empowerment Through the Bosnian Women's Initiative* (Geneva, 1999), 1.

33  S. Maguire, *A Family Affair: A Report of Research into Domestic Violence Against Women in Albania, Bosnia and Herzegovina, Croatia, and the Federal Republic of Yugoslavia* (Oxford: 1998), 22-28.

34  Lithander, *Engendering the Peace Process*, 44.

35  International Human Rights Law Group, *A National NGO Report on Women's Human Rights in Bosnia and Herzegovina* (Sarajevo, 1999).

36  International Rescue Committee (IRC), *Reproductive Health Survey* (Gorazde, 1999), 7.

37  IRC, *Reproductive Health Survey*, 7.

# Post-conflict Situation in *Kosovo*

June 11-16, 2001

## Background

### Historical Context

As wars overwhelmed the former Yugoslav Republics of Croatia and Bosnia and Herzegovina in the early to mid-1990s, the question for some analysts was not whether but when Kosovo* would become similarly embattled. Although the impoverished province was not as strategically critical to Serbia's hegemony as the recalcitrant Republics, Kosovo was at one time the heart of the Serbian Kingdom as well as the site of the Serbs' ignominious fall to the Turks, and it remained home to many of the most important Serbian Orthodox churches. Also home to an Albanian nationalist movement, Kosovo was reapportioned during World War II to form part of the briefly instated Greater Albania. At the end of the war, when Marshall Tito assumed control of Yugoslavia, Kosovo was rejoined with Serbia. Long-standing Albanian/Serb tensions escalated fitfully within Kosovo during Tito's regime, but Tito managed, as in other parts of socialist Yugoslavia, to quell resistance by granting Kosovo substantial autonomy. In Yugoslavia's constitution of 1974, Kosovo was retained as a province of Serbia, but it was granted its own government and courts, as well as federal representation in Belgrade.

This degree of independence served to heighten Albanian Kosovars' desire for autonomy, thus exacerbating ethnic polarities. After Tito's death and the subsequent resurgence of Balkan politics based on nationalism, Kosovo attempted in 1990 to secede from Serbia. Inspired by Serb leader Slobodan Milosevic, Belgrade's parliament responded by dismantling Kosovo's government and inserting a police state that excluded Kosovar Albanians from virtually all spheres of influence. Under the leadership of Ibrahim Rugova, Albanian Kosovars reacted in turn by creating parallel systems of governance, education, and enterprise. While a largely distracted Serbia engaged in wars with Croatia and then with Bosnia and Herzegovina, this system proceeded with relative success. In spite of ongoing human rights abuses, interethnic conflict did not escalate to civil war proportions. Nevertheless, organized military opposition to Serbian authority increased throughout the 1990s, especially after Kosovo was ignored in the Dayton Accords. Toward the end of the decade Serb forces were engaged in regular and reportedly brutal battle with the Kosovo Liberation Army (KLA) and the ethnic Albanian civilian population. International attempts to broker peace at the Rambouillet summit in Paris collapsed in March 1999 after Serbs refused to sign a peace agreement, acting instead to accelerate violence against ethnic Albanians in Kosovo, who by that time comprised some 80 to 90 percent of the total Kosovar population.

NATO responded by launching an air campaign against Serbia on March 24, 1999. During the three months of bombing and Serb advances, over one million Albanian Kosovars were displaced within or forced out of Kosovo. After Milosevic consented to withdraw his troops in June 1999, an interim United

* While the Serb spelling of *Kosovo* is used within this report in order to maintain consistency with international standards, all other geographic spellings are in Albanian in order to reflect common usage among the current majority population.

Nations Administration Mission in Kosovo (UNMIK) was established, vesting powers of governance in an internationally administered protectorate. NATO succeeded where Rambouillet had failed. For ethnic Albanians the offensive went beyond Rambouillet expectations by effectively cleansing Kosovo of the Serb population, as well as the Romas who were perceived to have assisted the Serbs. At the end of the war, Albanian Kosovar refugees repatriated in unprecedented flows: within two months 90 percent had returned to a countryside in which some 60 percent of houses had been burned and much of the infrastructure destroyed. Against this tide of returnees, most of the civilian Serbs and Romas who had not been killed or were not living in U.N.-protected villages generally escaped to either Serbia or Montenegro.

## Current Government

According to the conditions set forth at Rambouillet—which currently inform Kosovo's status, even though an accord was not signed by Serbia—Kosovo is once again an autonomous province of Serbia within the Federal Republic of Yugoslavia. In practice, Kosovo is governed by UNMIK and protected by U.N. security forces (the military arm, KFOR and the civilian police, CIVPOL). Under the direction of a Special Representative to the Secretary General of the United Nations, three administrative pillars comprise the major functions of UNMIK: the U.N. leads civil administration; the Organization for Security and Cooperation in Europe (OSCE) administers democratization and institution-building; and the European Union manages economic reconstruction. The United Nations High Commissioner for Refugees (UNHCR) initially had responsibility for a fourth pillar, humanitarian affairs, but has since reduced its presence and authority. Kosovars have been invited to participate in UNMIK's transitional government through a Joint Interim Administrative Structure (JIAS), consisting of an Interim Administrative Council (IAC), a consultative Kosovo Transitional Council (KTC), and twenty ministerial departments.[1]

## Status of Women

As in the negotiations at Rambouillet, Kosovar women are vastly underrepresented in positions of power within the transitional administration. The KTC's original incarnation had no women. Ironically,

when it was later enlarged and women's participation rose to 17 percent, its powers were simultaneously eclipsed by the predominant IAC, which only has one local female representative, a Serb.[2] Another position was created in the IAC to accommodate an Albanian female, but its observer status limits the position's influence. Of the twenty ministerial departments, each co-led by an expatriate and a Kosovar, only two are co-led by Kosovar women. In anticipation of October 2000 municipal elections, a 30 percent quota of female candidates was established. However, the quotas were weakly promoted, so that an average of only 8 percent of those elected to local assemblies during Kosovo's first elections were women.[3] UNMIK's Office of Gender Affairs (OGA) has launched several programs supporting the needs of women, including hiring an international consultant to assess and assist programming efforts related to violence against women. Still, the OGA is marginalized within UNMIK's hierarchy and is viewed by some as an ineffective voice of local women. No Kosovar women held senior positions within the OGA until 2001.

The absence of local women within UNMIK's administration fails to acknowledge the pre-existing strength and influence of local women's advocacy and organizations, as well as the long-standing presence of professional Kosovar women within both academic and service sectors. Ethnic Albanian women forcibly removed from professional positions at the outset of the Serbian police state were central to the success of Kosovo's consequent parallel structures. During Kosovo's protracted police state, at least eleven women's NGOs were active in promoting women's rights and welfare. At the height of ethnic conflict in the late 1990s, many Kosovar Albanian women also provided critical political and humanitarian support to the ethnic Albanian resistance.[4] In spite of a lack of recognition within UNMIK's power structures, a number of local women's organizations have succeeded in establishing their own voice within the new Kosovo. Increasingly, one of their organizing agendas has been the issue of GBV.

## Gender-based Violence

### During Conflict

During Kosovo's refugee exodus, the international press focused much of its attention on the plight of ethnic Albanian victims of sexual atrocities. On the one hand, the attention highlighted an issue more often ignored by the international community; on the other hand, a sensational approach sometimes undermined rather than reinforced survivors' rights to dignity and privacy. An often-noted example is that of a male health provider in an Albanian refugee camp inviting, via loudspeaker, women victims to come forward and complete a GBV questionnaire.[5] Although estimates of the numbers of Kosovar Albanian war-related rape and sexual assault survivors range from ten to thirty thousand, research mounted by international organizations such as Human Rights Watch, the Centers for Disease Control, and OSCE has been unsuccessful in identifying the real numbers of victims.[6] Even absent hard data on the numbers of women violated, research efforts have provided a general picture of the nature of Serb abuses: systematic rape, often by groups of police or paramilitary, often taking place over a series of days or weeks of forced sexual and domestic servitude. Most of the victims are thought to be women and girls under twenty-five years of age. Many were further brutalized with cuts to their breasts, legs, faces, and genitals. In rare instances, men also reported having been sexually assaulted.[7] No information exists on the extent to which Serbian women or ethnic minority Roma were exposed to sexual violence during and after the conflict.

Difficulty in estimating the prevalence of interethnic rape leading up to and during the NATO bombings has been attributed to the stigma of sexual violence. For some Albanian Kosovars rape is considered a fate worse than death. Perhaps especially in rural areas—where traditional patriarchal attitudes are stronger than in urban centers—disclosure puts survivors at risk of being rejected by their families and communities.[8] Still, fears of social stigma may be only one of several to inhibit reporting. Fear of exploitation by international and even local press may be another deterrent. In the wake of a stream of international press reports spotlighting sexual violence during the Kosovo conflict, a local literary magazine sought to publish firsthand accounts of women's rape experiences. Although they assured anonymity and were successful in collecting stories, many women subsequently withdrew their testimony for fear of exposure. Another local women's NGO attempted to survey its constituency but found that women were reluctant to repeat what they observed were the negative experiences of Bosnian women who had publicly revealed personal accounts of sexual violation.

Yet another possible obstacle to reporting is the lack of confidential psychosocial support available to GBV survivors. As a result of sexual violence assessments completed during and directly after the refugee crisis, the United Nations Population Fund (UNFPA) and the World Health Organization (WHO) made recommendations for comprehensive services. In addition, guidelines for prevention and response to sexual violence were published in Albanian and widely distributed by the Women's Commission for Refugee Women and Children. Still, there are few organizations in Kosovo providing counseling or health services to Albanian sexual assault survivors. Of those few, none has had extensive training in responding to sexual assault, and only one has provided services to non-Albanian women. However, there is some suggestion that affected women are receiving informal assistance in managing the effects of their victimization. According to a comprehensive report on violence against women published by UNIFEM in 2000, ethnic Albanian rape survivors sought the support and confidence of local women esteemed in their communities.[9] Within its limits, this informal network has indeed maintained the privacy of the women it informally assists.

## Beyond Conflict

In this culture of silence, there are ongoing incidents of rape. UNMIK police headquarters receives, on average, one report per day of rape throughout Kosovo, most often committed by gangs. A significant 18 percent of the women surveyed by UNIFEM acknowledged rape by men known to them, including boyfriends, husbands, and other family members.[10] UNIFEM's findings are all the more troubling given that marital rape is specifically excluded as a crime in Kosovo's existing legal code. Although there are no statistics on the percentage of cases of non-marital rape brought to trial, OSCE recently conducted a review of the judicial system. They found that in trials of violence against women, traditional perspectives that blame the victim and relegate violence to the private sphere prevail. In one trial open to the public, for example, an adolescent survivor of paternal incest testified that:

> She escaped from her father and ran away to her grandmother's house. The presiding

judge asked the victim, "When you went to your grandmother did you inform your father because under [customary] Albanian law you must tell your father?"...At one point, the victim started to tell the judge that what the judge was saying was untrue, but the judge cut her off and told her not to speak. Inexplicably, the presiding judge also asked the girl a number of questions as to "why" her father had raped her...During the lunch break, the victim was left alone in the courtroom, unattended, with the defendant, her father. At the conclusion of the trial, the defendant was acquitted.[11]

Given the existing culture and lack of support to victims, the prevalence of rape and sexual assault in Kosovo is impossible to identify, even more so among Serb and Roma populations. General information about domestic violence, however, is somewhat more accessible. The Center for Protection of Women and Children (CPWC) undertook research in 1996 which found that 68 percent of women interviewed acknowledged violence and that 70 percent of the perpetrators were family members.[12] UNIFEM's post-war assessment found that 23 percent of Kosovar Albanian women interviewed had experienced domestic violence in 1999 and 2000. The local women's organization Afrodita surveyed five hundred Kosovar Albanian men and women from the Ferizaj area of Kosovo in 2000 about perceptions of violence: 39 percent agreed that husbands beat wives; 90 percent identified the violence as physical.[13]

Local and international initiatives to address domestic violence have proliferated in the last two years. (It should be noted, however, that none of these initiatives target the minority Serb or Roma populations.) It is unclear whether the increased reporting of domestic violence incidents reflects the success of education and sensitization campaigns encouraging women to come forward, or an increase in the rates of violence. Several women's organizations providing client services believe the latter: that rates of domestic violence have escalated since the end of the war. One well-known women's organization, for example, served fifteen hundred survivors of violence from mid-1999 to mid-2000, but in the last half of 2000 served upward of two thousand cases.[14]

There is also concern about the increase in prostitution and trafficking of women. As early as September 1998, exploitation and prostitution of women and girls were recognized by the Kosovar women's community as potential consequences of the international community's presence. Even so, trafficking was not taken up by the international community until well after NATO bombing ceased. The province serves as both a final destination and a transit point for women being trafficked to Europe. Since February 2000 the International Organization for Migration (IOM) has provided return and reintegration assistance to 160 trafficked women, the majority of whom were recovered through police raids. Most were from Moldova, and over half were between eighteen and twenty-four years of age.[15] Informal estimates of total numbers of women trafficked into prostitution far exceed those who have received assistance. According to a UNMIK circular, "the fragility of the legal system has encouraged the development of organized criminal activity, of which prostitution is an integral component." Further, "the presence of the international community is also seen to provide a lucrative new market for prostitutes."[16] As with domestic violence, several programs have been initiated to address the prostitution of trafficked women.

Other potential forms of violence against Kosovar women and girls that have received less attention are sex-selective abortions and female infanticide. Legal in Kosovo, abortion is for some a primary form of birth control. In a household reproductive health survey conducted by UNFPA from November 1999 to February 2000, women acknowledged preferring sons at a rate 30 percent higher than daughters. UNFPA's findings suggest that the availability of ultrasonic technology may allow this preference to be actualized: "The sex ratio at birth has been consistently greater than the biological norm...There is seen to be a 95 percent probability that the excess masculinity among all births over the past ten years is significant ...Excess masculinity is always greater among the last-born child."[17] Another method of increasing the percentage of male children is the disposal of female babies. A representative of the consultative U.N. Office of the High Commissioner of Human Rights (OHCHR) has been informally monitoring female infanticide. Reports or rumors of a female baby abandoned to die average one per month. Although concerns have been expressed by international and local women about the possibility of sex-selective abortions and female infanticide, to date there have been no programmatic efforts to investigate further or directly address this issue.

## Current GBV-related Programming

It perhaps goes without saying that the lack of representation by and for women within UNMIK's power structures undermines Kosovo's ability to redress patriarchal traditions and associated GBV. Even so, local women's organizations are becoming a critical and articulate lobby for decrying gender inequities, including GBV. At the international level, an unprecedented number of humanitarian organizations have embraced the task of addressing GBV—particularly domestic violence and trafficking—either by initiating their own activities or by establishing partnerships with local NGOs. Although relationships among international and local organizations have sometimes been tense, especially in terms of allocation of resources, coordination, and shared decision-making, the combined efforts of local and international actors have nevertheless led to some exemplary successes in GBV programming. The successes are all the more remarkable given the setting, where few initiatives specific to GBV previously existed.

### Prishtinë

Several projects emanating from Prishtinë, Kosovo's capital, support or reinforce a significant portion of the work of field-based GBV programs throughout the province. The CPWC has since 1993 provided multiple services for women, especially survivors of GBV, including medical treatment, counseling, legal aid, and temporary shelter. With initial assistance from an Italian NGO and subsequent funding from multiple international donors, CPWC expanded its post-conflict operations to nine other cities throughout Kosovo, offering an admixture of health, psychosocial, and human rights services. Motrat Qiriazi is another long-standing organization currently serving women in four regions of Kosovo. The organization's director is a leading advocate of women's rights, responsible for coordinating Kosovo's Rural Women's Network among other activities. The Network's thirty-three local member organizations meet regularly in Prishtinë and are presently organizing an innovative media and cultural campaign against GBV that will produce popular songs, TV and radio spots, and a traveling theater group to raise awareness of and opposition to violence against women. The Network has also recently instituted an internet-based newsletter that is able to inform subscribers worldwide about activities related to women

in Kosovo. Yet another organization based out of Prishtinë working on issues of violence against women is the NORMA Women Lawyer's Association. NORMA led a roundtable discussion on domestic violence at the end of 2000 and is now participating in a working group to create laws specific to domestic violence, as well as conducting field-based seminars on women's rights, one aspect of which is domestic violence.

These major local organizations receive financial support from multiple sources. CPWC lists fifty-eight donors in its year 2000 report. Several of these donors are specifically committed to promoting gender equity and equality. One is the well-regarded Swedish organization Kvinna till Kvinna (KtK), working in Kosovo since 1994. KtK not only provides financial assistance to local organizations but also conducts advocacy activities, such as its publication critiquing UNMIK's gender approach. A much larger and more diffusely distributed source of technical and financial support comes from the Kosovo Women's Initiative (KWI), one of the first and primary post-conflict funders of Kosovar women and women-oriented organizations. With an initial $10 million grant in August 1999 from the U.S. Department of State's Bureau of Population, Refugees, and Migration, the UNHCR undertook management and distribution of KWI funds to international and local NGOs whose programming addressed the needs and rights of Kosovar women.

Although GBV prevention and response was a stated, if not primary, objective of KWI, support for GBV programming has not been strategically conceptualized, promoted, or coordinated by KWI, so that few of KWI's implementing partners have an exclusive mandate to address GBV. One important exception is the Women's Wellness Center (WWC) in the western town of Pejë. Implemented by the International Rescue Committee (IRC), the WWC offers GBV community sensitization and training Kosovo-wide, and direct counseling and referral services for survivors in the Pejë region. Another exception is KWI's one-time disbursement of funds to a Prishtinë-based shelter for trafficking victims that provides safe housing for women awaiting return to their countries of origin.

Even without a specific strategy to tackle GBV, KWI's support to organizations addressing women's health and psychosocial needs has indirectly facilitated GBV activities. For example, international implementing partners such as IRC, Mercy Corps International, and Relief International have conducted five-day reproductive health trainings for health care workers throughout Kosovo that include a GBV component. Local implementing partners that have received partial funding from KWI and that have also undertaken significant work on GBV include CPWC, NORMA, Motrat Qiriazi, and Radio 21.

In addition to providing financial support to implementing partners, KWI initially worked through "umbrella organizations" to distribute grants and technical assistance to small-scale women's projects. Although the early distribution of funds was fraught with logistical challenges, KWI has since streamlined its operation and is now moving toward a sustainable grants structure in which six local women's councils throughout Kosovo have responsibility for selecting and monitoring grantee organizations. The local women's councils receive administrative and technical assistance from IRC, which in 2001 became the lead agency for KWI's grants program. KWI currently supports over two hundred NGOs with start-up monies for programs that increasingly depart from the standard women's knitting and embroidery groups that constitute the bulk of KWI-supported activities. A small number of those initiatives, such as the Kodi women lawyer's association in Pejë, feature addressing GBV as an aspect of their organization's mandate. Other KWI-funded organizations have joined with existing GBV programs, such as the Pejë WWC, to conduct GBV sensitization to their staff and constituency.

In addition to UNHCR, other U.N.-level organizations have undertaken activities in the last two years that directly or indirectly support GBV programming. OSCE, for example, not only conducted a critical review of the judicial system's limited response to GBV (excerpted above), but also designed guidelines and facilitated brief trainings for local police officers regarding GBV legal statutes. The United Nations Children's Fund (UNICEF) is currently supporting CARE to run music concert events in six municipalities in Kosovo with the theme "Family Violence is a Crime: Think of Your Child." UNICEF also introduced GBV-trained triage nurses into several pilot hospitals throughout Kosovo so that women victims could be targeted and thus assisted with medical care and referrals more sensitively. In 2000, WHO conducted focus groups on violence, and WHO's gender focal point was responsible, in conjunction

with Mercy Corps International, for leading a coordination group of international and local NGOs to address domestic violence. UNIFEM published the first-ever assessment of GBV in Kosovo, *No Safe Place*, which is often used as the baseline for ongoing analysis on violence against Kosovar women. The UNMIK OGA subsequently hired UNIFEM's researcher as a consultant to review police reports on violence against women and work with CIVPOL in analyzing the implications of those reports. The OGA consultant also compiled a referral list of agencies and institutions providing support to survivors and spearheaded the first Kosovo-wide white ribbon campaign targeting men, entitled "Kosovar Men and Boys Against Violence Against Women," for which agencies throughout Kosovo developed media and other awareness-raising activities. In collaboration with local and international NGOs, the consultant designed and distributed a "Rapid Response Pack to Cases of Domestic Violence," to which the Department of Health and Social Welfare (DHSW) has added a standard GBV protocol for health care providers. Not insignificantly, the protocol was the very first of its kind issued by the DHSW and was a result of identified need based on the numbers of women reporting to the triage nurses trained and placed in select Kosovo hospitals by UNICEF.[18]

The U.N. High Commissioner for Human Rights (UNHCHR) has been a lead consultant to working groups charged with the task of drafting trafficking and domestic violence legislation. The trafficking legislation has been adopted and the domestic violence legislation is pending. In a further effort to counter trafficking, UNMIK issued an internal circular outlining a code of conduct for its staff, including a warning that UN immunity "may be waived in the event that staff are prosecuted for crimes relating to prostitution, including the use of sexual services of a victim of trafficking."[19] CIVPOL created a specialized anti-trafficking unit, and has more recently launched a domestic violence unit. CIVPOL has also been responsible, along with OSCE, for introducing training on GBV into the local Kosovo Police School curriculum.

The international NGOs operating in or from Prishtinë that have GBV components include IOM, CARE, International Medical Corps (IMC), OXFAM, and the STAR Network of World Learning. IOM has been a leader in addressing the issue of trafficking, both through monitoring activities, the findings of which are enumerated in locally distributed publications on trafficking, and through direct services to victims such as the Prishtinë safe house described above. IOM also participates in a multiagency working group on trafficking. In 2001, CARE developed and facilitated a three-day training for social workers on domestic violence, and is currently cooperating with local NGOs and OSCE to conduct community outreach forums and media campaigns throughout Kosovo. IMC has targeted youth for GBV education and also contributed, along with OXFAM, to the OGA's white ribbon campaign. OXFAM and the STAR Network continue to support local women's NGOs with training and capacity building.

## Kosovo-wide

Many of the Prishtinë-based organizations listed above have community awareness, training, and NGO capacity building programs that extend beyond the capital city. There are also several notable field-based organizations whose main activities target survivors. The above-mentioned service-mapping of the OGA consultant has made it easy to identify those organizations. In Prizren and Pejë, the UK-funded NGO One-to-One provides day shelter and counseling services for survivors, mostly domestic violence victims. The IRC-supported Women's Wellness Center in Pejë, which is currently moving from an internationally managed to an independent and locally managed NGO, provides counseling services to (mostly domestic violence) survivors, community education and outreach Kosovo-wide by mixed gender teams, and multisectoral professional training on GBV issues. In Gjakovë, Medica Mondiale has developed a comprehensive health and psychosocial program serving survivors of sexual and domestic violence, whose psychosocial program is exemplary for its ongoing staff training program. Gjakovë also has a Women's Association Shelter for domestic violence survivors that can accommodate fifteen women and children. Providers of free legal services for survivors exist in six regions of Kosovo: Medica Mondiale in Gjakovë, Liria in Gjilan, Kujtimi Foundation in Mitrovice, Kodi and CPWC in Pejë, Teuta in Prizren, and NORMA in Prishtinë.

## Summary

The list of GBV-related activities outlined above is, by any post-conflict standard, exceptional in its breadth. Organizations and institutions, as well as individual representatives from the local to the UNMIK level, are working to address GBV-related issues. Although most major initiatives are based in Prishtinë, many of their activities extend to other regions in Kosovo. Outside of Prishtinë, several projects focus specifically on GBV, and many others have included GBV sensitization and training as a component of their programming. One sure cause of this unusual flowering of GBV-related activities is the influence of local women's organizations that quickly regrouped following the end of NATO bombing; another is the attention paid by the media to the issue of war-related violence against Kosovar women; yet another is the sums of international money that flowed into post-war Kosovo, allowing humanitarian aid to extend beyond basic health response and infrastructure rebuilding.

Nevertheless, UNMIK's early failure to incorporate women into its power structures and to embrace gender as a basic building block of Kosovo's evolving government has meant that many of the above-listed "women's" activities are not centralized, which compromises their reach and impact. This lack of foresight by UNMIK may have long-term effects. The model recruitment and training program of the Kosovo Police Service (KPS) is a case in point. As a result of gender-sensitive recruiting, approximately 20 percent of the total number of KPS cadets are women. This unprecedented percentage of women, who with their male counterparts receive cadet training on GBV, has the potential to positively influence the application of GBV-related laws, as well as the ongoing effectiveness of the specialized trafficking and domestic violence units. However, the irregular response to violence against women by the overwhelmingly male CIVPOL international forces, who in turn are responsible for working with newly trained KPS officers, may undermine the GBV-related skills that KPS officers learn during training. The relative lack of gender awareness or existence of women in the CIVPOL forces could offset the potential advantages of the KPS gender-sensitive recruitment and training efforts.

Another significant limitation in addressing GBV at the government level is illustrated by the actions of the judiciary. As described in OSCE's report, GBV cases are rarely tried *in camera* (privately), and verdicts often favor the defendant.[20] Limited efforts have been made by UNMIK to train the judiciary in the application of laws. Legal organizations such as NORMA and Kodi may be able to conduct advocacy and facilitate the drafting and implementation of more gender-sensitive laws, but their efforts to provide counsel for women will be limited by the biases of judicial representatives and the courts' failure to apply statutory laws.

UNMIK's DHSW has made little effort to work with the network of government-operated centers for social work around the issue of domestic violence or sexual assault. (It is worth noting that CARE's brief training on domestic violence was the result of a request by social workers to receive information on these issues, thus suggesting a desire among social workers to gain expertise in the area of GBV.) Furthermore, UNICEF's nurse triage pilot program has not been comprehensively adopted by the DHSW, such that there is no government-based policy or plan to continue the triage services. And though the DHSW made a significant contribution to the "Rapid Response Pack to Cases of Domestic Violence" with its domestic violence protocol, the implementation of the protocol continues to be irregular and not well coordinated. Most coordination, in fact, is voluntary—based on the initiative of dedicated local and international organizations that have a priori embraced the issues of GBV. The government supports no multiagency or cross-sectoral coordination, which results in, on the one hand, limited local and national capacity for a comprehensive response to GBV and, on the other, an inevitable duplication of services.

Other limitations in GBV response include the province-wide lack of services for sexual assault survivors. Virtually all programming targets domestic violence or trafficking survivors, and only a limited amount of community education has focused on sexual violence. The culture of silence surrounding sexual violence remains, even though the local and international communities have introduced prevention and response activities to address other forms of GBV, and even though CIVPOL police reports suggest that sexual violence is an ongoing phenomenon.

Relative to sexual violence, the issue of counter-trafficking is well publicized and internationally supported, but programmatic funding remains erratic. IOM and the Prishtinë-based shelter for trafficked victims have had difficulties securing financial support to continue their shelter. In all of Kosovo, only two

other shelters exist for non-trafficked GBV survivors, with the capacity to serve a total of seventeen women and children. Although these shelters serve as models, they are not sufficient to address the needs of a population of two million.

Nor do current services sufficiently address the needs of minority groups or men. Several of the activities listed above include minorities in their client population, but because many programs are run by Kosovar Albanians, the likelihood of segregated minority populations—Serbs and Roma—being able to access services is slim. Similarly, with the exception of the white ribbon campaign, men are not targeted. There are no programs that specifically address male survivors or perpetrators of violence.

There are the foundations on which to build more comprehensive GBV programming in Kosovo. However, as donor funding decreases in accordance with Kosovo's transition from emergency to development, GBV initiatives may be among the most at risk. A case in point is the Women's Wellness Center in Pejë: funded for two years by KWI under the IRC, it is now struggling to find ongoing financial resources to function as a local NGO and risks losing its experienced staff if it cannot maintain its pay scale. Now that the emergency phase has passed, international donor funds are increasingly limited—especially for local NGO projects—and the government is not yet financially able to provide monies to most social service activities or organizations. If the government is to assume the task of supporting programming to address GBV, it will require the continued support of international donors, both in terms of direct aid and aid to existing local women's NGOs that can provide the government with expertise to address the issues of GBV.

## Recommendations

1. International donors must continue to seek out and support programming to address GBV. Short-term self-sustainability should not be a requisite of donor support. Priority funding should be given to expert local NGOs that are currently working in the area of GBV, and that can assist the national and local governments to further institutionalize plans and protocols to address GBV.

2. Efforts should be made to institutionalize the activities of the OGA into all permanent government ministries. In particular, the national government should support the multiagency coordination activities instituted by the OGA, to ensure comprehensive response by all actors, including police, judiciary, and NGOs. An inter-agency working group should be established at the government level. Efforts should be made to incorporate the expertise of NGOs currently working in the area of GBV as advisors and facili-tators of coordination activities.

3. The government should institute shelter pro-grams in the major regions throughout Kosovo, ensuring the safety of client and staff by includ-ing KPS in shelter activities.

4. UNMIK should immediately undertake to train CIVPOL forces in standard responses to GBV, not only to ensure the rights of survivors but also to enable CIVPOL officers to serve as on-the-ground trainers for the incoming KPS.

5. UNMIK should improve its ability to monitor the KFOR and CIVPOL contributions to pros-titution and trafficking and apply the related anti-trafficking regulations. Regional coordina-tion should be established with counter-trafficking efforts throughout the former Yugoslavia and other countries of origin in Eastern Europe.

6. The Ministry of Justice should regularly review the statistics collected by the specialized trafficking and domestic violence units, and a sexual assault unit should be similarly established and monitored. As was recommended by the OGA consultant, separate interview rooms should be created in police precincts to facilitate interviewing and ensure confidentiality for survivors.

7. The DHSW should institute UNICEF's pilot nurse triage project in all hospitals throughout Kosovo. The hospitals should also be adequately equipped with forensic medical equipment, and forensic doctors should receive comprehensive training in collecting evidence and providing tes-timony in GBV cases. The government's network of centers for social work should be trained in meeting the case management, support, and referral needs of survivors. Social workers should also be trained to provide support to survivors negotiating the judicial system. The DHSW should be responsible for instituting, collecting, and monitoring GBV-related health and social services statistics.

8. The Department of Justice should ensure that judges and lawyers are informed of the laws relat-ing to GBV, and should monitor the prosecution of GBV cases. The Department of Justice should also undertake community education campaigns about the revision of GBV-related laws.

9. The service-mapping report of OGA should be translated into the local language and distributed to all relevant service providers.

10. Specific programs should be initiated to address the particular needs of minority populations and men.

# Notes

1    C. Corrin, *Gender Audit of Reconstruction Programs in South Eastern Europe*, The
     Urgent Action Fund and the Women's Commission for Refugee Women
     and Children (New York, 2000), 4.

2    International Helsinki Federation for Human Rights, *Human Rights in the
     OSCE Region: The Balkans, the Caucasus, Europe, Central Asia and North America,
     Report 2001* (Vienna, 2001), 514.

3    Kvinna till Kvinna (KtK), *Getting It Right?: A Gender Approach to UNMIK
     Administration in Kosovo* (Sweden, 2001), 5-15.

4    B. Byrne, R. Marcus, T. Powers-Stevens, *Gender, Conflict, and Development,
     Report No. 35*, Bridge Development-Gender (Sussex, 1995), 54-56.

5    D. S. Fitamant, *Evaluation Report on Sexual Violence in Kosovo*, Report for
     United Nations Population Fund (UNFPA) (Geneva, 1999), 8.

6    See Office of Security and Cooperation in Europe (OSCE), *Background
     Report on Kosovo: As Seen, As Told* (Prishtinë, 1999); Human Rights Watch,
     *Kosovo: Rape as a Weapon of Ethnic Cleansing* (New York, 2000); M.Hynes and
     B. Lopes-Cardozo, "Sexual Violence Against Women in Refugee Settings",
     *Journal of Women's Health and Gender-based Medicine*, 9, no. 8 (2000): 819-824.

7    R. Wareham, *No Safe Place: An Assessment on Violence Against Women in Kosovo*,
     UNIFEM (Prishtinë, 2000), 23.

8    Fitamant, *Evaluation Report*, 8.

9    Wareham, *No Safe Place*, 72.

10   Wareham, *No Safe Place*, 37.

11   OSCE, *A Review of the Criminal Justice System: February 1, 2000- July 31, 2000*
     (Prishtinë, 2001), 80.

12   Center for Protection of Women and Children (CPWC), *Annual Report
     2000* (Prishtinë, 2001), 3.

13   Cited in: C. Clark, "Gender-based Violence Research Initiatives in
     Refugee, IDP, and Post-Conflict Settings: Lessons Learned" (draft paper to
     be presented at the Global Health Conference, Washington, D.C., 2002),
     10.

14   CPWC, *Annual Report 2000*, 6.

15   International Organization for Migration (IOM), *Return and Reintegration
     Project: Situation Report, February 2000-May 2001* (Prishtinë, 2001), 3.

16   U.N. Administration Mission in Kosovo (UNMIK), Circular 4 (2001): 1.

17   UNFPA, *Demographic, Social, and Economic Situation and Reproductive Health in
     Kosovo following the 1999 Conflict: Results of a Household Survey* (Prishtinë,
     2001), 57.

18   U.N. Interim Administration, *Department of Health and Social Welfare Health
     Care Protocol 1/2001* (Prishtinë, 2001), 1.

19   UNMIK, Circular, 1.

20   OSCE, *A Review of the Criminal Justice System: February 1, 2000-July 31, 2000*
     (Prishtinë, 2001), 86.

Country Profiles from
Latin America

*Colombia*
*Guatemala*
*Nicaragua*

# Internally Displaced in
# *Colombia*

A Desk Study Overview by Melinda Leonard

## Background

### Historical Context

Colombia has the distinction of being one of Latin America's most stable democracies in spite of a prolonged internal conflict. Fighting began in 1948, soon after a change in power from the Liberal to the Conservative party, marking the start of a two-decade period referred to as "La Violencia." Throughout the 1950s and 1960s, violent demonstrations against the government were countered with repressive state measures, particularly in rural areas, leaving more than 300,000 civilians dead and forcing an estimated two million people to flee to cities.[1] Numerous guerilla groups emerged in the 1960s, most notably the Fuerzas Armadas Revolucionarias de Colombia (Revolutionary Armed Forces of Colombia, or FARC) and the Ejército de Liberación Nacional (National Liberation Army, or ELN). Colombia's drug trade also began to develop in the 1960s, starting with marijuana and expanding to cocaine. Drug trafficking gave rise to drug lords and cartels, which in turn led to a new breed of violence committed by paramilitary forces organized to protect drug traffickers' interests. An era of "narco-terrorism" defined the 1980s and 1990s. Paramilitaries, who formed a nationwide association known as the Autodefensas Unidas de Colombia (United Defense Groups of Colombia, or AUC), were increasingly aggressive in their attacks on civilians, including politicians and members of the judiciary.[2] The effects of the protracted conflict have been particularly serious for women: a local women's group has reported that more than 360 women are killed annually as a result of political violence.[3]

The current coalition government, lead by Andrés Pastrana, has engaged in numerous rounds of talks with the rebel paramilitary forces, though little progress has been made, and fighting continues in approximately 515 of Colombia's 1,000 municipalities. Currently, rebels have a strong presence throughout the country and control a large area in central Colombia known as "the demilitarized zone." In 2000, Pastrana's administration requested assistance from the international community through an aid package, "Plan Colombia," designed to address the narcotics business, socioeconomic development, human rights, and the country's insurgency. The United States has committed military resources to Colombia as part of this plan, primarily to support a "war on drugs."[4] There is concern among human rights organizations that U.S. military aid could lead to an escalation of the armed confrontation.

The length of the conflict has resulted in a culture of pervasive impunity, largely because of a breakdown in the judicial system. Criminal organizations have targeted magistrates through violent attacks with the result that perpetrators are seldom held responsible for their actions. In addition to these successful intimidation tactics, corruption is widespread. Police officers and state agents have been accused of participating in drug-related massacres and other human rights abuses against civilians.[5] Human rights advocates have become targets because of their denunciation of the violence. Hina Jilani, the United

Nations Special Representative of the Secretary General on Human Rights Defenders, visited Colombia in October 2001 to investigate incidents relating to violence against human rights activists; her initial findings indicate a pattern of abuses including threats, disappearances, killings, and forced displacements. Women's groups have also received threats from paramilitary groups. For example, a facility providing services for women in Barrancabermeja run by the Organización Feminina Popular (Popular Women's Organization, or OFP) was destroyed in November 2001 by paramilitaries who had made threats to the organization in March.

## Internally Displaced

A by-product of the violence has been the massive internal displacement of approximately two million Colombians since 1985, an estimated 49 to 58 percent of whom are women.[6] Fighting between the army, guerrillas, and paramilitary groups has forced entire populations of some villages to flee their homes and abandon their property. Between 30 and 50 percent of internally displaced persons (IDPs) are concentrated in large cities and surrounding areas,[7] primarily Bogotá, Medellín, Cartagena, and Cali. Additional settlements exist in rural areas throughout the country, including extremely remote mountain regions. The widespread absence of state control often leaves IDPs with few protections and limited access to basic services such as education and health care. Although the government has passed laws ensuring protections for IDPs, such as access to emergency humanitarian aid, guarantees of safety, and the right to health care, a lack of implementation resources undermines the delivery of those protections. Government regulation requires that IDPs register with the Red de Solidaridad Social (Social Solidarity Network, or RSS) in order to receive emergency aid, but the number of registration centers is limited and the registration process is not confidential. As such, many IDPs are reluctant to seek government aid. The Consultoria para el Desplazimiento Forzado y los Derechos Humanos (Consultant for Forced Displacement and Human Rights, or CODHES), a local organization that works with the Catholic Church and other NGOs to produce statistics on displacement in Colombia, estimates that only 40 percent of IDPs are registered.

Registered or not, displaced persons are often stigmatized by and excluded from the communities where they settle, suffering discrimination by public agencies and state services.[8] Living conditions are sometimes deplorable: many settlements in and around Colombia's major cities are overcrowded and have inadequate sanitation and water, as well as limited access to schools, work opportunities, and shopping centers.[9] Difficulties in getting an education and finding work are one explanation for the rise in adolescent girls' participation in armed groups and gangs. Lack of health care services is another source of vulnerability for IDPs. In 2001, the Asociación Probienestar de la Familia Colombiana (PROFAMILIA) conducted interviews with project staff in clinics providing health services to IDPs and found that many displaced women have never heard of sexual and reproductive health,[10] in part because affordable care is not available. Recent studies have shown that adolescent girls displaced by the conflict have the highest level of pregnancies among girls in poor communities.[11]

## Status of Women

Discrimination against IDP women occurs in the larger context of widespread gender inequities. Despite constitutional guarantees ensuring equality between the sexes, women must demonstrate higher qualifications than men when applying for the same jobs, and yet earn an estimated 28 percent less than men.[12] Women have a higher rate of unemployment than men; if employed, women are more often engaged in subsistence labor, particularly in rural areas.[13] Although women are statistically well represented in the government's central administration, holding 59 percent of all posts, they occupy only 19 percent of directorships in the administration,[14] underscoring their under-representation in positions of influence. Despite recent improvements in the legal status of women—part of far-reaching policy reforms aimed at increased democratization and modernization[15]—the enforcement of those laws remains limited. This failure to support women's rights is of particular concern with regard to the prevention of and response to GBV, especially in the case of IDPs.

## Gender-based Violence

### Conflict-related

In November 2001, the United Nations Special Rapporteur on Violence against Women visited

Colombia to investigate the effects of the conflict on women. In a statement following her investigation, she highlighted the need to bring to light "invisible acts" of GBV, such as the rape of women before they are killed. Estimates cited by the Special Rapporteur indicate that approximately 84 percent of human rights violations against women are committed by paramilitaries, 12 percent by guerrillas, and 3 percent by state actors.*

Sexual violence is systematically used against Colombian women and girls as a tactic to destabilize the population. Armed groups have reportedly kidnapped girls as young as five years old and raped them. These incidents are generally unreported, and authorities often do not investigate or even note the rapes of women who are found murdered. [16] Ironically, girls may join armed factions in order to avoid sexual abuse, domestic violence, or maltreatment in their homes, but the patterns of abuse are often continued in the armed groups. [17] Former girl combatants have reported incidents of sexual violence by their superiors; they also report limitations to their rights that include forced abortions or forced use of contraception. [18]

Even if not active combatants, women and girls sometimes choose or are encouraged by their families to develop attachments with paramilitaries as a form of protection. A 2001 delegation to Colombia sponsored by the Women's Commission for Refugee Women and Children found evidence of girls as young as twelve engaged in relationships with members of armed groups. In one case, a sixteen-year-old was killed by her paramilitary boyfriend. [19] Although a sexual relationship with a paramilitary can initially be an honor, additional anecdotal data from the Women's Commission delegation indicates that it may put girls at greater risk of being attacked or killed by opposing groups. The Women's Commission draft report includes a case of the murder of a fourteen-year-old girl in Putumayo who was the sister of a guerrilla but lived with a paramilitary and was suspected of spying. [20] Prostitution among IDP girls is increasing as the conflict continues, with reports of paramilitaries offering money for sex to girls as young as eleven and twelve. Information obtained by the Women's Commission delegation suggests that IDP girls turn to prostitution as a means to support their families, who in some cases prostitute their daughters.

Trafficking in women is also increasing. Colombia is currently the third most common country of origin for trafficked women, with as many as 35,000 victims ending up in Europe and Asia each year. [21] The Hope Foundation, an NGO working on the issue of trafficking in Colombia, has attributed the rise in trafficking to the ongoing conflict and the displacement of millions of people, as well as the lack of laws that specifically address trafficking. [22] According to the organization's founder, increasing numbers of Colombian women are arriving over the border in Ecuador, where they are being recruited by international crime rings to travel to third countries to work as prostitutes. [23]

Beyond Conflict

The conflict-related violence against women takes place against a backdrop of high GBV prevalence rates and underreporting throughout Colombia. An estimated 34 women per 100,000 were the victims of sexual crimes in 1995. [24] There were a total of 13,703 cases of probable rape reported in 1999, despite the prevailing culture of secrecy that inhibits disclosure. [25] It has also been estimated that there are 775 rapes of adolescents annually, with only 17 percent of victims publicly denouncing the acts. [26] While they likely suffer greater exposure to violence, reporting rates among displaced women is similarly low; in a 2001 survey of women displaced by armed conflict, 84 percent of those interviewed had never looked for help after being mistreated. [27]

Laws related to the prevention and protection of rape and sexual violence have improved, even if enforcement remains weak. In 1996 rape in marriage was made a criminal offense, and in 1997 the Penal Code provision that a rape offender could be exculpated from liability if he married the victim was repealed. The attitudes of judges in cases of violence against women contribute to the problem of successful prosecution, in that subjective judgments are often made based on the "reputation" of the woman, who is more often considered not to be a credible witness. [28] Other obstacles to reporting acts of rape include a requirement that all forensic evidence must be taken by a doctor from the government's forensic medicine department, and many survivors cannot afford to pay the fees for laboratory tests needed for investigations. As a result, many women are hesitant or unable to make use of the criminal

---

* Following the visit of the Special Rapporteur, additional independent experts visited Colombia to assess the impact of conflict on women and women's role in the peace process. Their findings will be published in a UNIFEM-sponsored global report in early 2002.

justice system for assistance in protecting and enforcing their rights.

Domestic violence in Colombia is considered to be a private matter. The Colombian Institute of Family Welfare estimates that 95 percent of all abuse cases are not reported.[29] The new Law on Family Violence, passed in 1996, criminalized spousal rape for the first time and provided legal recourse for victims of family violence.[30] However, like the laws protecting women from non-spousal rape, the domestic violence laws are not well enforced. The Human Rights Ombudsman's 1999-2000 report characterized intrafamily violence as an "increasing problem."[31] The Institute of Legal Medicine documented an average of ninety-three cases of domestic violence per day in 1994; this number increased by 40 percent in 1997.[32] Displaced and marginalized women are at particularly high risk of domestic violence. In a survey conducted in 2000 by PROFAMILIA, 50 percent of those interviewed had been physically abused by their partners.[33] Statistics indicate that domestic violence is underreported among both displaced and non-displaced populations.

## Current GBV-related Programming

The government of Colombia has taken numerous steps to denounce violence against women and has passed progressive legislation to promote GBV programming. Revised family violence laws require that victims of domestic violence have access to shelters and that therapeutic counseling is offered to perpetrators. Current law also provides for municipal Family Protection Councils where victims of domestic abuse can go for support. However, lack of resources and government commitment to enforce laws has hampered the implementation of these provisions, particularly in areas with high concentrations of IDPs. As a result, most of the work being done to address violence against women in IDP communities is being undertaken by U. N. institutions and local and international NGOs.

At the national level, the United Nations Population Fund (UNFPA) is collaborating with various governmental agencies, including the national police and municipal administrations, to develop norms for an integrated and multisectoral response to sexual violence. The goal is to ensure that victims of sexual violence receive assistance that recognizes and pro-

motes their fundamental rights to justice, health, protection, and education. This model project—which has yet to be fully implemented—will be evaluated in May 2002 and eventually expanded into a national program through the government of Colombia. UNFPA and the United Nations High Commissioner for Refugees (UNHCR) have also supported local NGOs' GBV-related activities. For example, UNHCR recently funded the Bogotá-based organization Casa de la Mujer to conduct a workshop on domestic violence that included community rights, legislative issues, and self-awareness exercises.

Another GBV programming area with both governmental and nongovernmental support is community education and public awareness-raising. Centro de Recursos Integrales para la Familia (Center for Integrated Resources for the Family, or CERFAMI) in Medellín has published and distributed a twelve-page pamphlet entitled *If She Says No, It's Rape*. The pamphlet offers a definition of rape, information on supportive services, and guidelines for reporting procedures. The Office of the Mayor of Bogotá has a similar campaign using billboards to promote family commissaries as a place to report incidents of violations of children's rights, including sexual violence. The commissaries are a part of the larger structure of the Colombian National Family Welfare system, which includes the Colombian Institute for Family Welfare. However, the billboards appear to be limited to Bogotá, and there is no indication of a national campaign, nor is there any way to measure the campaign's reach or impact with regard to IDPs. In fact, none of the programs mentioned above specifically target the displaced. Given that IDPs are often living in remote areas or are reluctant to seek services because of security issues, this lack of targeting likely means that programming fails to reach a large percentage of the IDPs, who may be at highest risk of GBV.

PROFAMILIA has undertaken to bring sexual and reproductive health services to displaced women throughout the country. It runs perhaps the most targeted of IDP programs with GBV components: a health education project that includes workshops focusing on domestic violence and direct services for victims such as routine gynecological examinations and counseling. Legal assistance for women is also provided by PROFAMILIA in six cities around the country; the programs aim to educate women about their rights under the Convention on the Elimination of All Forms Discrimination Against Women and to provide advice on legal options in situations of family and other violence. PROFAMILIA has set up forty-six clinics in thirty-two cities in Colombia, and has a rural program that covers eleven out of a total of twenty-six provinces in the country, using mobile clinics and counselors to reach populations that might otherwise receive no assistance. Despite their successes, the dangerous climate that still pervades the country, particularly in many displaced communities, has made it difficult for PROFAMILIA to operate in certain areas. Doctors and health care workers are increasingly vulnerable to attacks and kidnappings. As a result, PROFAMILIA has had to devise creative strategies for ongoing service provision, such as transporting displaced persons to clinics or arranging educational activities in less dangerous areas. And PROFAMILIA is not yet reaching the most remote and rural parts of the country, where local and IDP women have virtually no access to health care or educational workshops.

## Summary

Widespread violence continues to threaten all sectors of the Colombian population, placing IDPs and women at particular risk. Although the Colombian government has made progress in addressing the needs of the internally displaced and women in general, inadequate resources and a lack of a coordinated effort have stalled initiatives to redress GBV. In addition, the government is not providing sexual and reproductive health services; discrimination against women is pervasive; and perpetrators enjoy a culture of impunity. Beyond implementing basic programming to improve the general welfare of IDPs, basic data on the incidence and prevalence of violence against IDP women will be critical to the development of any efforts to limit the high rates of sexual crimes and intrafamily violence.

At present the efforts of local and international NGOs to prevent and respond to GBV remain largely localized, with most work conducted in urban settings. The Colombian government's legislation aimed at improving the legal status of women is largely unenforced, and efforts by local and international NGOs have not yet been sufficient to counter the prevailing traditions that support violence against women. The targeting of human rights defenders and health care workers further limits the capacity of local and international organizations to provide even the most basic services in remote areas, where IDP women and girls may be at greatest risk for violence.

Given the current financial crisis resulting from Colombia's internal emergency, the international donor community should commit to work with the government in the design and implementation of GBV prevention and response activities for IDPs. Such support will allow the government, in turn, to collaborate with local expert NGOs and members of the IDP community to develop GBV-related programs that address the needs of IDPs in both urban and rural settings. For example, protocols may be introduced for GBV-related health and psychosocial care.

The international human rights and aid community should also assist the government in exercising the laws that are designed to protect against GBV. To this end, it will be critical to train judicial and law enforcement staff on issues of GBV. Additionally, international, government, and local initiatives should facilitate the widespread dissemination of information relating to women's rights and GBV-related protections available under Colombian law.

## Notes

1 Women's Commission for Refugee Women and Children, *A Charade of Concern: The Abandonment of Colombia's Forcibly Displaced* (New York, 1999), 3.

2 A. Tirado Mejia, "Violence and the State in Colombia," in *Colombia: The Politics of Reforming the State*, ed. Eduardo Posada-Carbo (New York, 1998), 121.

3 *El Tiempo* (Bogotá), 15 Nov. 2001.

4 M. Chernick, "The Dynamics of Colombia's Three Dimensional War" *Journal on Conflict, Security and Development* 1, no. 1 (2001): 93-100.

5 Tirado Mejia, "Violence and the State in Colombia," 118.

6 United Nations, "Internal Displacement Situation" (unpublished report of the Thematic Group on Internal Displacement, Bogotá, August 2001), 13.

7 Women's Commission for Refugee Women and Children, *Unseen Millions: The Catastrophe of Internal Displacement in Colombia* (New York, 2002).

8 Women's Commission, *Unseen Millions*, 2002.

9 Women's Commission, *Unseen Millions*, 2002.

10 Asociación Probienestar de la Familia Colombiana (PROFAMILIA), "Monitoring Report" (unpublished report of Project Providing Sexual and Reproductive Health for Internally Displaced Populations in Colombia, February 2001).

11 Women's Commission, *Unseen Millions*, 2002.

12 U.S. Department of State, Bureau of Democracy, Human Rights, and Labor, *Colombia Country Report on Human Rights Practices, 2000* (Washington, D.C., 2001).

13 U.S. Department of State, *Colombia Country Report on Human Rights Practices, 2001*.

14 Organization of American States (OAS), *Third Report on the Human Rights Situation in Colombia* (Washington, D.C., 1999).

15 Committee on the Elimination of All Forms of Discrimination Against Women (CEDAW), "Colombia," (Concluding observations/comments, February 4, 1999), 5.

16 Women's Commission, *Colombia Delegation Report*, 2002.

17 Terre des Hommes, "Girls in the Colombian Armed Groups" (A Diagnosis Briefing, Osnabrück, Germany, September 2001), 12.

18 Terre des Hommes, "Girls in the Colombian Armed Groups," 15-16.

19 Women's Commission, *Colombia Delegation Report*, 2002.

20 Women's Commission, *Colombia Delegation Report*, 2002.

21 T. Pratt, "Sex Slavery Racket a Growing Concern in Latin America," *Christian Science Monitor*, 11 Jan. 2001.

22 U.S. Department of State, *Colombia Country Report on Human Rights 2000*.

23 Pratt, "Sex Slavery Racket a Growing Concern in Latin America."

24 OAS, *Third Report on the Human Rights Situation in Colombia*, 230.

25 U.S. Department of State, *Colombia Country Report on Human Rights, 2002*, 57.

26 OAS, *Third Report on the Human Rights Situation in Colombia*, 230.

27 PROFAMILIA, "Violencia contra las mujeres y los ninos" (unpublished document, Bogotá, 2000), 114.

28 Center for Reproductive Law and Policy, *Reproductive Rights in Colombia* (New York, 1998), 18.

29 U.S. Department of State, *Colombia Country Report on Human Rights*, 2002, 57.

30 U.S. Department of State, *Colombia Country Report on Human Rights*, 2002, 58.

31 U.S. Department of State, *Colombia Country Report on Human Rights*, 2002, 57.

32 Center for Reproductive Law and Policy, *Reproductive Rights in Colombia*, 19.

33 PROFAMILIA, *Salud Sexual en Zonas Marginales: Situación de las Mujeres Desplazadas* (Bogotá, 2001).

# Post-conflict Situation in *Guatemala*

A Desk Study Overview by Melinda Leonard

## Background

### Historical Context

For nearly half a century the small Central American nation of Guatemala has been rife with political violence, suffering five coups and numerous coup attempts. Conflict first escalated to civil war proportions in 1954 when increasing pressure by the United States and its allies forced elected president Jacobo Arbenz to resign. The government was overtaken by a military junta, and a long period of oppressive rule ensued, during which opposition rebel forces and guerrilla groups emerged.[1] Determined to end military rule, the main guerrilla factions united in 1982 to form the Unidad Revolucionaria Nacional Guatemalteca (Guatemalan National Revolutionary Unit, or URNG). Guatemala's military dictator at the time, General Rios Montt, responded to the consolidated opposition with a counterinsurgency campaign. The campaign's "scorched earth" tactics, involving massacres and forced displacements, resulted in over four thousand civilian deaths during 1982 and 1983. Government forces have, in fact, been credited with nearly 94 percent of all human rights abuses and acts of violence committed after the outbreak of internal strife.[2] An estimated 500,000 to 1.5 million Guatemalans were displaced or fled to neighboring Mexico during the years of conflict.[3] The majority fled between 1978 and 1985, the most concentrated period of violence.

Peace talks began in 1991 under the leadership of President Jorge Serrano and then accelerated in 1996 under President Alvaro Arzu Irigoyen. In April 1996 the URNG declared a unilateral cease-fire, and in December the civil war came to an official end with the signing of final peace accords. The accords set high standards for the transition to democracy and for the rebuilding of society.[4] They also included numerous agreements on human rights, including women's rights. The signing of the accords stimulated the return of Guatemalan refugees from Mexico. Between 1994 and 2000, 43,000 refugees were repatriated. The United Nations Verification Mission (MINUGUA) was charged with monitoring the human rights mandates of the peace accords.

The government has considerably improved its human rights record, though problems remain. MINUGUA reported in 1999 that failures in the administration of justice and public security were causing widespread fears of further violence among the civilian population.[5] A 2000 visit by the United Nations Special Rapporteur on the Independence of Lawyers and Judges exposed a justice system suffering from ongoing corruption, lack of resources, and threats to its judges and lawyers. Another recent concern of human rights advocates is the possibility of "social cleansing" of suspected criminals—extrajudicial killings or torture by vigilante groups frustrated by the state's failures to prosecute crimes.[6] Despite the army's history of participation in human rights violations, the government has enlisted its help in order to supplement the National Civil Police's failed attempts to maintain a sense of security.[7]

## Status of Women

The civil war has had a profoundly negative impact on the women of Guatemala—exposing them to torture and sexual abuse, causing widespread displacement, leaving an estimated 120,000 widowed,[8] and sending the country's maternal mortality rate to a high 200 deaths per 100,000 live births.[9] Conversely, the war has contributed to women's visibility at the national level. Although Guatemalan women remain underrepresented in political leadership, holding only 13 of 113 Congressional seats,[10] the post-accords government has set up a number of agencies devoted to women's issues, including an Office for the Defense of Women in the Attorney General's Office for Human Rights and the newly formed Coordinator for the Prevention of Domestic Violence and Violence Against Women. Other important women's groups within the governmental structure are the National Women's Forum, which links the government and local women in the design of national policy, and the National Permanent Commission for the Rights of Indigenous Women. Although these institutions suggest increased commitment on the part of the government to address women's issues, few if any government efforts have been targeted at acknowledging and ameliorating the effects of widespread violence experienced by Guatemalan women during the years of conflict.[11]

Civil sector programming for women, as well as Guatemala's feminist movement, strengthened during and following the conflict, in part because of the work of local and international NGOs. Women who were displaced by fighting to camps along the Mexican border participated in educational workshops on gender and human rights led by the United Nations High Commissioner for Refugees (UNHCR) and international implementing partners. Refugee women also participated in women's groups and established alliances that informed the development of local women's organizations following the post-accords refugee repatriation. The largest and most influential local women's NGO was Mama Maquin, which organized forums for women to articulate their concerns about return to Guatemala. Mama Maquin has continued to be active on behalf of returned refugee women despite threats and at least one documented case of an attack on members by unidentified men urging the women to give up their efforts to promote women's equality.[12] Another organization that grew out of the refugee experience is the

Coordinadora Nacional de Viudas Guatemala (National Coordinating Group of Guatemalan Widows, or CONAVIGUA). The group has a broad platform of objectives that involves pressuring the government to pass laws of protection for widows and mothers; making the voices and demands of widows heard in political, economic, and social dialogue; and helping Guatemalan women—particularly indigenous women in rural areas—to become involved in Guatemala's political and social reconstruction. Other secular and religiously affiliated women's groups cover issues from human rights and reproductive health to agrarian reform. It is primarily these local initiatives that, with the assistance and support of international activists, are addressing issues of GBV.

## Gender-based Violence

### During Conflict

Women in Guatemala lived under a pervasive threat of sexual violence during the country's long civil war.[13] Sexual violence was commonly used by counterinsurgency forces during the 1980s: women were kidnapped, tortured, and raped by the military.[14] A 1982 study cited by researcher Virginia Rich found that the overwhelming fear of most female Guatemalan refugees was that of being raped.[15] Perpetrators acted with relative impunity, committing sexual assaults that were so widespread in the highland combat zones one local official commented that it would be difficult to find a Maya girl of eleven to fifteen who had not been raped.[16] Rape was used as a tactic to bring shame and guilt into the community. Traditional values among Maya women prevented victims from seeking help after sexual assaults; and because of their "silent suffering," many survivors endured chronic gynecological problems and psychological trauma.[17]

Despite an anecdotal consensus that war-related sexual violence was prevalent, virtually no research has been conducted to assess the nature and scope of that violence. Most evidence comes from projects initiated to investigate and document allegations of broad-based human rights abuses. Testimonies of victims gathered throughout Guatemala by the Recuperation of Historical Memory Project of the Office of Human Rights of the Archbishop's Office of Guatemala (REMHI) confirm that women were not only forced to watch the abuse and killing of family members, but were also themselves victims of sexual torture and sexual slavery.[18] The 1998 REMHI report documented cases of violations committed by the military against both individuals and groups of women. In many cases, sexual violence accompanied massacres, thus adding to the challenge of assessing the total number of rape victims.

The U.N.-sponsored Guatemalan Commission for Historical Clarification (CEH) published similar testimonies documenting over 42,000 human rights violations, the majority perpetrated by state forces and paramilitaries during the thirty-six-year civil war. The 1999 report reveals rape as a common practice, especially but not exclusively targeting Maya women. CEH findings indicate that survivors of sexual violence still suffer profound trauma, including feelings of shame and fears of recrimination from the state agents who perpetrated the violence.

The experience of women who fled to refugee camps in Mexico was significantly more positive in terms of protection from and services for GBV. UNHCR, in collaboration with international humanitarian aid organizations, offered programs on gender, reproductive health, and human rights. Many refugee women participated in self-awareness workshops aimed at reinforcing their self-esteem and promoting empowerment. Legal claims against fellow refugees for sexual harassment, rape, and domestic violence increased in the refugee camps as women became more willing to report.[19] However, gender sensitization did not extend to men in the camps. As women's networks set up in the camps were disrupted following repatriation, many women resumed subordinate status within their families and communities.[20]

Since the peace accords, the Guatemalan government has responded to the reports of conflict-related sexual violence by reiterating the president's request that Guatemalans forgive the state for acts committed during the war. The URNG similarly acknowledged excesses without admitting to a deliberate strategy of mass rape and sexual assault of civilians. This failure by political actors to address the GBV suffered for decades by Guatemala's women has likely reinforced traditions that discourage survivors from seeking assistance.[21]

## Beyond Conflict

Obstacles to reporting GBV exist as well outside the context of Guatemala's civil war. Guatemala's laws governing rape are prejudicial against women, placing the burden of proof on the victim. The Penal Code requires that violence must be evident in order to prosecute rape, which discourages many victims from coming forward. Police are typically ill trained and ill equipped to investigate cases, and even when charges are lodged, a rapist can be exonerated under Guatemalan law if he marries a victim over the age of twelve.[22] Not surprisingly, few rape cases go to court, and even fewer end in convictions. Unofficial statistics indicate that in 1999 only 80 out of 323 reported rapes were successfully prosecuted.[23] Failure to report incidents of criminal sexual violence is assumed to be widespread,[24] though there are no official statistics on underreporting.

Traditions that inform the perpetuation of sexual violence also contribute to spousal abuse. Domestic violence is deeply rooted in Guatemalan society, as evidenced by the expression, "He who loves you beats you."[25] An exploratory study on attitudes toward domestic violence conducted in 1993 by the Guatemalan Ministry of Public Health and Social Assistance found that many government officials in a position to address domestic violence held traditional victim-blaming perspectives.[26] Findings also indicated that Guatemalan women with all levels of education and from all social classes were at risk of abuse.[27] As with rape, underreporting is widespread, and successful prosecutions are rare. Official statistics for the first ten months of 1999 recorded 1,664 complaints of domestic violence and yet only 28 convictions from all cases.[28]

## Current GBV-related Programming

Although the government created several organizations and agencies dedicated to women's development as part of the 1996 peace accords, those specifically addressing the issue of violence against women are few. One is a hotline created specifically for domestic violence survivors run by the Guatemala Secretary of Public Works' Program for the Prevention and Eradication of Intra-Family Violence. Additionally, MINUGUA is involved in a project with the Guatemalan Judiciary and the Ministry of Education to promote confidence in state institutions and the application of justice. The program, intended for the indigenous population and designed to combat the growing vigilante justice problem, includes workshops on topics such as public responses to violence and training on legal codes.[29] The program does not specifically address the issue of violence against women, but increased confidence in the judicial system may encourage women to seek assistance in cases of GBV.

Among the most effective programs are those organized by NGOs. For example, Asociación Mujer Vamos Adelante (Association for the Advancement of Women, or AMVA) specializes in education and training on women's rights and public participation. Founded in 1992, AMVA's goals are to strengthen the role of women in Guatemalan society by training female community workers to lead rights-based workshops in rural areas, where there is an appreciable lack of programming on women's issues.

Several local and international NGOs are working in the health sector to address the needs of Guatemalan women, though most programs do not specifically address the issue of violence against women. The local affiliate of the International Planned Parenthood Federation, the Asociación de Pro-Bienestar de la Familia de Guatemala (Association for the Well-Being of the Family, or APROFAM) offers counseling services to help raise women's self-esteem as part of its larger goal of providing integrated family planning and maternal and child health care. A hotline set up by APROFAM for sexual and reproductive health information receives approximately 40 percent of its calls from domestic violence victims, despite the fact that the hotline was not originated to address this issue.

The only health program that specifically targets returnee women was informed and inspired by work with Guatemalan refugees along the Mexico border. Initiated and facilitated by Marie Stopes International, the program is designed to combat Guatemala's high maternal mortality rate by bringing education and services to returnee communities in the vicinity of Huehuetenango, Guatemala. The program is based on findings by Marie Stopes that many returnees in northern Guatemala were crossing back into Mexico to take advantage of the health services available in refugee camps that were not available at home. Marie Stopes further identified intrafamily violence as one of the vulnerabilities to women's health in Guatemala. The project's education activities therefore include sensitization about issues related to domestic violence, particularly its increase during pregnancy.

Another area of focus for NGO-initiated programming is community education. The local Myrna Mack Foundation is working on a project to disseminate information contained in the REMHI report through community-based human rights education. Although the program does not target GBV, many of the testimonies from the REMHI report contain accounts of sexual violence. Distribution of the testimony creates greater community awareness and dialogue about GBV. Unidas Para Vivir Mejor (United to Live Better, or UPAVIM), a small organization comprised of around sixty-six women living in a squatter settlement in Guatemala City, has identified spouse and child abuse as a major social problem and offers education and personal development programs as part of its campaign to improve quality of life among its constituents.

## Summary

The long civil war in Guatemala featured among its human rights abuses a high frequency of GBV by state actors, though real numbers are impossible to obtain given the stigma associated with reporting and the overall lack of services to survivors. Societal attitudes that discouraged public revelations of sexual crimes, as well as the relative impunity afforded perpetrators, was not a discrete phenomenon of the war: even today, a conspiracy of silence regarding GBV is the norm, and relatively few programs exist to address its prevention or to provide adequate response to survivors. The utility of the recently instituted hotlines for victims of domestic violence illustrates the need for further programming specifically dealing with GBV. However, no programs can be effectively designed without improving methods for GBV data collection, for which there appears to be no national policy or plan.

Moreover, there does not appear to be a large-scale effort to deal with the lasting trauma of survivors of sexual violence as distinct from the general violence of the civil war, nor to help communities understand and support survivors more effectively. Programs focusing on the culture of violence and the sensitization of the population about the issue of GBV will be fundamental to promoting healing and combating the ongoing prevalence of GBV.

Educational activities with refugees and returnees along the Mexican border have illustrated the capacity of local women's groups to organize, but there is little technical or financial support available to returnee women—especially in rural areas. As such, many of the gains produced by the empowerment activities that were a component of camp-based education and training have since been overshadowed by a resumption of traditional gender roles that subordinate women. Even so, the activities of some of the women's NGOs listed above may be supported to include programming that more aggressively addresses GBV as a fundamental violation of women's rights. The several national women's institutions that exist to address the welfare of women are also resources for further stimulating GBV prevention and response programming.

## Notes

1   P. Calvert, *Guatemala: A Nation in Turmoil* (Boulder, Colo., 1985), 113.

2   U.S. Department of State, *Guatemala Country Report on Human Rights Practices*, Bureau of Democracy, Human Rights, and Labor (Washington, D.C., February 2001).

3   V. Garrard-Burnett, *Aftermath: Women and Gender Issues in Post-conflict Guatemala*, U.S. Agency for International Development (USAID), Center for Development Information and Evaluation, Working Paper No. 311 (September 2000), 3.

4   Garrard-Burnett, *Aftermath*, 4.

5   U.N. Verification Mission (MINUGUA), *Ninth Report on Human Rights in Guatemala* (Geneva, 1999), 3.

6   MINUGUA, *Eighth Report on Human Rights in Guatemala* (Geneva, 1998), 3.

7   MINUGUA, *Eighth Report on Human Rights in Guatemala*, 4.

8   University of Sussex Institute of Development Studies, *Guatemala: Fighting for Survival Against Militarism*, Development and Gender Brief, Issue 3 (June 1996): 1.

9   International Planned Parenthood Federation, *Guatemala Country Profile* (London, 1999), 4.

10   U.S. Department of State, *Guatemala Country Report on Human Rights Practices*, 26.

11   Garrard-Burnett, *Aftermath*, 9.

12   U.N., *Report of the Special Rapporteur on Violence Against Women, Its Causes and Consequences* (Geneva, 1999), 2.

13   V. Rich, *Gender Violence in Guatemala* (Brussels, forthcoming), 1.

14   Garrard-Burnett, *Aftermath*, 5.

15   Rich, *Gender Violence in Guatemala*, 1.

16   Rich, *Gender Violence in Guatemala*, 2.

17   Garrard-Burnett, *Aftermath*, 6.

18   Oficina de Derechos Humanos del Arzobispado de Guatemala, *Guatemala: Never More* (Guatemala, 1994), 2:27.

19   S. García, "Outside, Looking In," *Refugees* (June 1, 1995): 5.

20   Garrard-Burnett, *Aftermath*, 11.

21   Garrard-Burnett, *Aftermath*, 6.

22   International Society for Human Rights (ISHR), *Law and the Status of Latin American Women* (Frankfurt, 2000), 2.

23   U.S. Department of State, *Guatemala Country Report on Human Rights Practices*, 26.

24   U.S. Department of State, *Guatemala Country Report on Human Rights Practices*, 26.

25   ISHR, *Law and the Status of Latin American Women*, 2.

26   Ministerio de Salud Pública y Asistencia Social Estudio Exploratorio, *Violencia intrafamiliar hacia la mujer en Guatemala* (Guatemala City, 1993).

27   Estudio Exploratorio, *Violencia intrafamiliar*.

28   U.S. Department of State, *Guatemala Country Report on Human Rights Practices*, 27.

29   "State, MINUGUA Join Forces to Curb Lynchings," *Cerigua Weekly Brief* 24 (June 25, 1999): 1.

# Post-conflict Situation in *Nicaragua*

A Desk Study Overview by Melinda Leonard

## Background

### Historical Context

A victim of the cold war, Nicaragua is still struggling to overcome the political and economic instabilities wrought by years of internal conflict. In the early 1960s, the Sandinista Front for National Liberation (FSLN or, commonly, the Sandinistas) was created as a populist-based political movement to unify opposition to the U.S.-supported Somoza dynasty—a family dictatorship that forcibly assumed power in 1936 and was sustained by three generations of Somozas. The Soviet-supported Sandinistas, characterized by militant nationalism and a unique version of Marxism-Leninism, mounted a guerrilla war that in 1979 succeeded in overthrowing the Somozas' forty-three-year regime.

However, the legacy of poverty resulting from the Somozas' personal usurpation of Nicaragua's resources, as well as rising tensions with the United States, undermined the Sandinistas' struggle to institute the socialist policies that were the platform of their revolution. The Contras, an opposition movement trained and financed by the U.S. government, spread throughout rural Nicaragua. The ensuing "second wave" of civil war raised the military and civilian death toll to an estimated 80,000, further ravaging an already fragile infrastructure and economy. Although the conflict came to an official end in 1990 with the election of Violeta Chamorro as president, sporadic fighting between mercenary groups that grew out of the remains of the Contra movement still occurs in rural areas.

The transfer of power from the Sandinistas to Chamorro was initially collaborative—to the extent that the Sandinistas controlled the National Assembly and the military during a four-year period of "co-government." When the period of co-government ended, Sandinista cooperation with the Chamorro administration decreased; few pieces of legislation were passed by the Sandinista-dominated Assembly, and political progress stalled. The early promise of Arnoldo Aleman, who peacefully succeeded Chamorro in 1996 and offered hope for an end to the Sandinista block, was soon overshadowed by allegations of corruption. The Aleman government's structural adjustment policies further concentrated wealth in the ruling classes, exacerbating already widespread poverty. The election of 2001 that brought former vice-president Enrique Bolanos to power has also stimulated concern that the corruption of Aleman's administration will continue, even as Nicaragua moves forward in its transition from conflict to development.

### Status of Women

Although overwhelmingly Catholic Nicaragua has a long history of conservative patriarchy, women's roles shifted during the Sandinista period. Women comprised 30 percent of the guerrilla force. The first Nicaraguan women's group, the Asociación de Mujeres Ante la Problemática Nacional (Association of Nicaraguan Women Confronting the National

Problem, or AMPRONAC), was formed in 1977 to provide civilian support to the Sandinista platform. Women actively participated in the early Sandinista government; they also benefited from literacy and health campaigns, as well as from inclusion in cooperatives and unions. Quasi-governmental organizations such as the Asociación de Mujeres Nicaragüenses Luisa Amanda Espinoza (Association of Nicaraguan Women "Luisa Amanda Espinoza," or AMNLAE) were developed to target specifically the needs of women, and their work included advocating for legal reforms as well as national health and literacy campaigns.

Despite the post-Sandinista evolution of such government institutions as the Nicaraguan Institute for Women, the National Committee Against Violence, and the Panel of Women and the Girl, a return to more conservative values during Chamorro's rise, coupled with a decrease in women's public representation, resulted in a commensurate decrease in national attention to issues of women's rights. Subsequent governments have upheld this conservatism. An Aleman administration proposal created a new Ministry of the Family to replace the Nicaraguan Institute for Women as overseer of women's programs. The proposal received heavy criticism from women's groups because of its statements promoting the traditional nuclear family and discriminating against families headed by single mothers and common-law couples.[1]

The massive destruction of Hurricane Mitch in 1998 further eroded women's standard of living, already on the decline as a result of post-civil war economic policies instituted by the Chamorro administration. Despite having predominated in the bureaucratic labor force during the Sandinista period, women now make up an estimated 88 percent of the poor in Nicaragua.[2] Structural adjustments by the Chamorro administration resulted in widespread elimination of public sector jobs, and the job market for women has thus declined drastically.[3] For those women who are employed, salaries are typically lower than those of men with comparable professional experience and education, with men making twice as much as women in some cases.[4]

In a climate of relative conservatism and gender inequity, the feminist movement that consolidated during the Sandinista period continues to be active in promoting and responding to women's concerns.

Although the movement is now primarily based in the civil sector rather than in the government, it has enjoyed considerable success in efforts to include GBV on the national agenda.

## Gender-based Violence

Sexual assault was reportedly an element of Nicaragua's years of conflict, particularly targeting indigenous communities, but no data has been published about the extent and nature of crimes committed. However, data do provide evidence that sexual violence became an endemic feature of post-conflict Nicaragua, exacerbated by men returning from the war to a weak economy and high rates of unemployment. The post-war phenomenon of violence against women was formally recognized in 1992, when Nicaragua hosted a National Conference for Women in which GBV was identified as one of the main problems facing Nicaraguan women. Between 1990 and 1994, the number of reported rapes rose by 21 percent, and the number of reported attempted rapes increased by 27 percent.[5]

Legislation introduced by Chamorro's administration instituted laws establishing rape as a public crime. Although the legislation made it possible for the state to charge a perpetrator, its reach was severely limited: laws did not apply to husbands; they allowed for paternity rights for rapists; and sentences were as short as nine months. Laws governing rape in marriage have since been reformed to establish stricter sentences for perpetrators, yet protections for victims of non-spousal rape and sexual abuse remain limited. The National Police listed 1,181 complaints filed by women concerning rape during 2000, and a total of 1,367 rapes were reported in 1999.[6] Despite this evident increase in reporting, official complaints are widely believed to under-represent the pervasiveness of the problem; women remain reluctant to come forward because of the stigma attached to rape.

Aside from the limitations in existing legislation, another precipitant to the continued high incidence of sexual crimes and their underreporting is the failure of the Nicaraguan government to enforce protections for potential victims and prosecute perpetrators to the full extent of the law. However, the climate for prosecuting sexual abuse may improve as the result of recent action taken in a high profile case: in 2001 the Inter-American Commission on Human

Rights agreed to hear a case brought by the step-daughter of former Nicaraguan president and Sandinista leader Daniel Ortega alleging sexual abuse. The case has stalled because a Nicaraguan court refused to lift the immunity that protects Ortega as a current member of Congress. The Commission is expected to rule on whether the Nicaraguan government failed to provide adequate judicial recourse for the complainant.[7]

The issue of domestic violence was also recognized in the 1992 National Conference for Women as a concern for post-conflict Nicaragua, though no statistics were then available to describe the extent of the problem. A landmark 1995 study conducted with La Red de Mujeres Contra la Violencia (Women's Network Against Violence, or WNAV) found that one out of every two women had been abused by their husband or companion at some point, and one out of three had been forced to have sex.[8] A later study by the Nicaraguan Statistics and Census Institute found that two out of ten women had experienced physical or sexual violence from a partner in the past year.[9]

In response to these alarming findings, and as a result of the lobbying effort of women's organizations, the government has introduced legislative protections for women exposed to domestic violence. The Law Against Aggression Against Women passed in 1996 made domestic violence a crime, punishable by sentences of up to six years, and established a system for the issuance of restraining orders for victims fearing further acts of violence. Moreover, a 1997 Penal Code reform instituted a prohibition against all forms of violence in families, including physical and psychological violence. In addition to these protections, both the government and the nongovernmental community have introduced various programs to address GBV. In fact, a 1998 periodic report of the U.N. Convention on the Elimination of All Forms of Discrimination Against Women (CEDAW) acknowledged the emergence of Nicaraguan NGOs and the development of governmental initiatives as positive steps in confronting the issue of violence against women.[10]

## Current GBV-related Programming

The post-Sandinista governments have responded to the issue of domestic violence with a variety of pro-

tections. After the 1992 National Conference for Women, in which GBV was recognized as a component of Nicaragua's post-war society, a number of government institutions and local NGOs took up the issue of violence against women. According to the United Nations Development Program (UNDP), several governmental-level agencies created programs specifically addressing GBV, including an Intra-familial Violence Program under the Ministry of Health and a Consultative Council on Gender within the National Police Force, responsible for specific GBV policies. Another important government initiative is a nationwide network of eighteen Commissariats for Women and Children, also referred to as Women's Centers, supported by the official Nicaraguan Institute for Women. Taking a multisectoral approach involving police, the judicial system, and NGOs, the Women's Centers provide specialized attention to those who register complaints of violence. The Women's Centers also run media awareness and prevention campaigns aimed at educating the population about legal codes related to GBV.[11]

Despite this evidence of increasing government attention to GBV prevention and response, most of the long-standing programming has been the result of action by local NGOs. One of the most widespread NGO initiatives to emerge from the 1992 conference is the WNAV. The organization is made up of over 150 local groups and several hundred individual members located throughout the country. Activities range from domestic violence sensitization and denunciation projects to public campaigns and lobbying efforts. WNAV also runs centers providing services for battered women. Advocacy efforts of members were central to reforming the penal code regarding domestic violence. In 1995 WNAV organized a national conference that brought five hundred women from professional groups, the police, grassroots organizations, and government institutions together to discuss domestic violence. At the conference they distributed booklets that provided practical listings of supporting agencies as well as an analysis of laws and social values that leave violence against women unchecked. The conference attracted significant media attention to the issue of domestic violence.[12]

Perhaps most in the vanguard with regard to GBV programs is the Asociación de Hombres Contra la Violencia (Association of Men Against Violence, or

AMAV). Founded in 1993 as the Group of Men Against Violence, the organization became a national association in 2000 in order to unite local groups throughout the country. The goal of AMAV is to reduce violence against women by confronting issues of masculinity and aggression. The organization seeks to educate and sensitize men regarding patriarchal traditions, gender equality, power, and GBV. In addition to coordinating the network of Men Against Violence groups, AMAV offers training workshops on machismo and violence, promotes alliances with women's groups (particularly WNAV), supports men's reflection groups, and participates in public awareness campaigns addressing issues of masculinity and violence. The organization stresses a need for men and women to reach decisions by consensus and focuses on developing skills for more positive and constructive listening and discussion between the sexes. AMAV has over one hundred active members throughout the country who participate in local and national activities. Another organization that has addressed the issue of masculinity is the Centro de Comunicación y Educación Popular (Popular Education and Communication Center, or CANTERA), which runs workshops around the issue of masculinity and popular education. With support from a variety of international partners, CANTERA offers educational programs and publishes books, reports, and short stories addressing a wide scope of issues, including masculinity and violence, cultural models, and masculine identities.

Puntos de Encuentro (Common Ground), a partner of the international development NGO One World Action, provides an example of a broad-based approach to the issue of GBV. Among its activities, the organization publishes the newsletter *Boletina*, organizes programs addressing psychosocial issues for individuals and groups affected by natural and social trauma, offers courses on capacity building for women's groups, and conducts public awareness campaigns addressing GBV. When research undertaken by the organization revealed that domestic violence had increased in the aftermath of Hurricane Mitch, Puntos de Encuentro launched a campaign in conjunction with the WNAV and AMAV with the tagline "Violence against women is a disaster that men can avoid." The campaign uses leaflets, informational brochures, posters, and radio and television announcements to publicize GBV-related issues, including anger management for men. Puntos de Encuentro also manages a documentation center for

information related to feminism, masculinity, violence, sexuality, youth, and institutional development, and has televised a program aimed at adolescents and their families dealing with sexuality, reproductive health, domestic violence, and other important issues facing youth in Nicaragua. The international organization MADRE has also participated in GBV programming, working in rural areas with the local NGO Wangky Luhpia to institute health clinics for women that offer counseling to victims of sexual abuse as a component of their services.

## Summary

Although sexual violence committed during Nicaragua's conflict is difficult to determine given the lack of data, policies, or programming, what is clear is that Nicaragua was subject to a general increase in GBV following from the devastation of years of war. There does not appear to have been a significant international response to the issue of GBV either during the conflict or directly afterward. Such a response may have been helpful in preventing the trend toward conservatism regarding GBV in early post-conflict administrations. International support also could have consolidated the initial gains of women's organizations that were born during the years of conflict and facilitated an early response to GBV, which was quickly identified by the women's community as an aspect of post-war culture.

Nevertheless, the evolution of the women's movement that was initially a strong component of the Sandinista revolution has led over time to great strides in institutionalizing GBV prevention and response activities. Empowered by their collaboration and inclusion in the Sandinista administration, women have worked to improve gender equity on issues ranging from land reform to protection of human rights. Prompted by the consistent lobbying activities of feminist organizations, the government of Nicaragua has recently made significant efforts to address the issue of GBV. The improvements in legislation and the introduction of government initiatives provide a basis from which to advance ongoing prevention and response activities.

However, there remains a lack of governmental will to implement legislation guaranteeing protections against GBV. Despite laws criminalizing domestic violence, women remain unlikely to press charges, and when victims do take perpetrators to court, most receive a verdict of not guilty because of a weak judicial system with little experience dealing with GBV.[13] Data on the prevalence of GBV remains difficult to obtain. Absent efforts by the government to collect and analyze such data, monitoring of GBV is difficult, as is the development of policies and programs to address the issue more effectively. Coordination between governmental agencies and the NGO sector also appears weak, undermining the effectiveness of programs designed to address GBV.

Government Women's Centers are a positive example of collaboration between government agencies and NGOs, and may be utilized as a model to expand GBV-related programming throughout the country. The programs targeting men represent some of the most innovative in the world and should be adapted to other conflict-affected populations. Perhaps most critically, the international aid community should continue to support the efforts of the government and local NGOs to ensure that the important gains achieved in addressing GBV continue to result in more effective and comprehensive initiatives.

Notes

1   J. Webster, "Women's Organizations Under Attack in Nicaragua," El Aviso (Winter 1996-7).

2   Social Watch, Country Report 2000: Nicaragua (Montevideo, Uruguay, 2001).

3   K. Isbester, Still Fighting: The Nicaraguan Women's Movement, 1977-2000 (Pittsburgh, 2001).

4   U.S. Department of State, Nicaragua Country Report on Human Rights Practices, Bureau of Democracy, Human Rights, and Labor (Washington, D.C., 2001).

5   Isbester, Still Fighting, 157.

6   U.S. Department of State, Nicaragua Country Report.

7   Inter-American Commission on Human Rights, Organization of American States, Report No. 118/01 (Washington, D.C., 2001).

8   United Nations Development Program (UNDP), Situation of Gender-based Violence Against Women in Latin America and the Caribbean: National Report Nicaragua (New York, 2001).

9   Isbester, Still Fighting, 214.

10  Committee on the Elimination of All Forms of Discrimination Against Women (CEDAW), Fourth Periodic Report of Nicaragua to the CEDAW (Geneva, 1998).

11  CEDAW, Fourth Periodic Report of Nicaragua.

12  Isbester, Still Fighting, 160.

13  U.S. Department of State, Nicaragua Country Report.

# Annex: Travel Schedule

The Africa, Asia, and Europe country profiles included in this report represent information obtained during site visits that were conducted in 2001 according to the following schedule.

| Date | Location | Participants |
|------|----------|--------------|
| January 22-31 | Republic of Congo | Jeanne Ward |
| February 5-15 | Sierra Leone | Jeanne Ward |
| February 18-28 | Rwanda | Jeanne Ward |
| April 14-21 | Pakistan | Jeanne Ward |
| April 22-29 | Thailand | Jeanne Ward |
| May 7-14 | East Timor | Jeanne Ward |
| June 3-10 | Azerbaijan | Jeanne Ward<br>Suzanne Petroni<br>Cari Clark |
| June 11-16 | Kosovo | Jeanne Ward<br>Cari Clark |
| June 18-27 | Bosnia and Herzegovina | Jeanne Ward<br>Cari Clark<br>Betsy Kovacs |

The desk studies of Colombia, Guatemala, and Nicaragua were undertaken in New York by Melinda Leonard during the fall of 2001.

Funding
U.S. Department of State,
Bureau of Population,
Refugees, and Migration

Design
David A Zilkowski

Photograph
David Turnley
© David & Peter Turnley/CORBIS.com

Printing
The Print Extension, Inc.
New York, NY

 Printed on Recycled Paper